POSH

PANCAKES

POSH
PANCAKES

Over 70 recipes,
from hoppers to hotcakes

Sue Quinn

Photography by Faith Mason

quadrille

Publishing Director: Sarah Lavelle
Creative Director: Helen Lewis
Copy Editor: Corinne Masciocchi
Editor: Harriet Butt
Series Designer: Gemma Hayden
Designers: Nicola Ellis and Emily Lapworth
Recipe Writer: Sue Quinn
Photographer: Faith Mason
Food Stylist: Emily Kydd
Prop Stylist: Alexander Breeze
Production: Vincent Smith and Nikolaus Ginelli

Published in 2018 by Quadrille, an imprint of Hardie Grant Publishing

Quadrille
52–54 Southwark Street
London SE1 1UN
www.quadrille.com

Cataloguing in Publication Data: a catalogue record for this book is available from the British Library.

ISBN: 978 1 84949 803 6

Printed in China

CONTENTS

INTRODUCTION

Who doesn't love pancakes? Thin and delicate, or thick and squidgy. Bite-sized or generously proportioned. Rolled, folded, or piled into towers. Drenched in syrup or stuffed with vegetables. Breakfast manna or superlative supper. Whatever your tastes or gustatory requirements, there's something for everyone in pancake land.

Researchers believe that as far back as 30,000 years ago, humans were partial to a pancake stack. Stone Age cooks mixed together ground-up plants and water, and fried the resulting batter on hot rocks greased with woolly mammoth lard. That last bit's made up, of course, but you get the picture; pancakes are almost as old as cooking itself. Why have they survived the test of time? Probably because they're cheap, and this vast food family shares one defining feature: flatness. It makes them easy to prepare, portable when necessary, and a versatile vehicle for almost any ingredient a cook has to hand. That's why virtually all cuisines have a version, from yeasty *injera* in the Horn of Africa to *pannekoek* in Holland.

These days, most of us know pancakes as stars of the breakfast table, a morning staple in some parts of the world, a daybreak treat in others. Served American diner-style, with bacon and an amber puddle of syrup, pancakes deliver the flavour-bomb triumvirate of salt, sugar, and fat. But there's so much more to pancakes than that. Stuffed with meat and baked under a blanket of gooey cheese, pancakes are the ultimate comfort food on a cold day. Plied with leafy greens and topped with an egg, they can be a nutritionally complete light meal. Studded with sweet or savoury morsels, and then baked until puffed and golden, pancakes transmogrify into something entirely different.

Whatever your personal preference, pancakes are relatively simple to make in their elemental form, with just a few basic ingredients required. There is a certain knack to getting them just right, but raw interiors, burnt exteriors, and chronic pancake stickage can easily be overcome with practice, the right kit, and by bearing a few basics things in mind.

A well-seasoned or non-stick griddle or frying pan, cast iron if budget allows, can really make the difference between pancake heaven and pancake hell. Keeping a vigilant eye on the heat, turning it up or down as required, will also enhance the chances of pancake perfection. And, of course, a well-seasoned batter that's just the right consistency is key to making them flavoursome and delicious. Notwithstanding this advice, the first pancake in a batch will invariably fail, especially when making crêpes. This is just the will of the pancake gods and is not, in fact, a problem. The scrappy mess that is your first pancake is the tester, the chance to get the heat just right. It's also a sublime cook's treat, to be eaten very hot and sprinkled with sugar straight from the pan.

It makes sense that we should all master how to make pancakes. Almost everyone loves them because they're flipping delicious. Onwards to the batter!

TIPS FOR PERFECT
★
PANCAKES

EQUIPMENT

A griddle or shallow frying pan
ideally made from well-seasoned or
non-stick cast iron is perfect for frying
pancakes. Some people believe you
need a specialist crêpe or omelette
pan for thin and lacy French-style
ones, but you don't. What you want is
a solid flat base that distributes heat
evenly, ideally with shallow sloping
sides. Most of the recipes in this book
are made in a frying pan with a base
measuring 16cm (6in) in diameter.

A large, flat heatproof spatula,
like the kind used to flip fish or eggs,
is pretty much essential for turning
large pancakes over. A palette knife
is also useful for getting under
the edges.

A whisk is perfect for stirring
together ingredients and removing
lumps, but a wooden spoon is fine.

A sieve is commonly used to sift
flour and other ingredients for
pancakes, but it's debatable whether
doing this makes much difference
to the end result. It's easier to use a
whisk to combine and aerate the dry
ingredients, but the choice is yours.

A 60ml measuring cup (2fl oz/¼
cup) is useful for scooping out just
the right amount of batter to make
pancakes of perfect equal size.

COOKING TIPS

Mixing:

Don't over mix pancake batter: it will develop gluten and the pancakes will be tough. The best way to avoid this is to whisk together the dry ingredients in a mixing bowl first and mix the eggs and other wet ingredients in a jug. Pour the wet ingredients into a well in the centre of the dry ones, stirring as you go to slowly incorporate the flour mixture from the sides. This way, much of the combining has already been done by the time the wet and dry ingredients get together, and avoids beating. A few small lumps are fine in thick pancake batter, but crêpe batter should be smooth.

Resting:

Resting crêpe batter for 30 minutes or so before cooking definitely yields a lighter, more even texture. This is because resting allows the starch molecules to swell, air bubbles to disperse, and any gluten formed while mixing the batter to relax. That said, your crêpes will still be perfectly okay if you omit this step. Don't rest batter for thick American-style pancakes, as the raising agents start working as soon as the wet and dry ingredients are mixed together, and your pancakes might not rise well.

The fat:

Adding melted butter or oil (not olive oil!) to the batter isn't essential, but imparts flavour and helps to make pancakes tender and prevents them sticking to the pan. Choose whichever you prefer: butter is tastier but tends to burn more easily. When frying crêpes, use only a tiny bit of melted butter or vegetable oil in the pan – a wodge of kitchen roll is ideal for applying and wiping out any excess. Thicker pancakes can do with a bit more fat for frying to ensure they're golden.

The heat:

Finding the correct heat to fry pancakes takes practice, depends on your hob and pan, and how you prefer your pancakes cooked. However, for thick pancakes, a medium heat works well: this ensures the bottom doesn't burn before the inside is cooked. Spoon a little batter into the pan and if it sizzles immediately, the temperature is about right. When bubbles start to form on the top of your pancakes, take a peek at the bottom and if golden, flip. Crêpes are best fried more quickly over a medium–high heat; the bottom should be golden just as the top is set.

Flours:

Different flours impart their own textures and flavours, so experiment. Start by substituting 25 per cent of the standard wheat flour in a recipe with options like coconut, buckwheat, wholemeal, rye, polenta, and gluten-free, and go from there. You might need to add a little more liquid to your batter.

Add-ins:
Try mixing a small handful of berries, dried fruit (chopped if large), chocolate chips, sliced banana, grated fruit (pear, apple, peach, and the like) into plain batter for extra pancake joy.

Keeping them warm:
Pancakes are best eaten warm, straight from the pan. However, if you're making thick American-style pancakes in a batch, you can stack them between layers of greaseproof paper or kitchen roll, and keep them in a low oven. Avoid keeping crêpes in the oven as they tend to dry out.

PANCAKE

★

BASICS

BUCKWHEAT

BLINIS

These diddy pancakes are traditionally served in Eastern Europe to mark the start of Lent, but they make fab canapés any time of year. Full of a yeasty, buckwheaty flavour, blinis are perfect vehicles for smoked fish, cream cheese and – of course – caviar.

 MAKES 40 blinis

 TAKES 40 minutes,
plus 2 hours resting

60g (2oz/½ cup) buckwheat flour
100g (3½oz/¾ cup) strong white
  flour
1 tsp salt
½ tsp caster (superfine) sugar
7g fast-action dried yeast
150ml (5fl oz/¾ cup) whole milk
200g (7oz) soured cream
2 free-range eggs, separated
melted butter or vegetable oil,
  for frying

In a large mixing bowl, whisk together the flours, salt, and sugar. Sprinkle over the yeast.

Heat the milk in a small pan until warm, but not hot – you should to be able to dip your finger in without it burning. Remove from the heat, and whisk in the soured cream and egg yolks. Pour the milk mixture into the flour mixture and stir to make a thick batter. Cover with clingfilm (plastic wrap) and leave to rest in a warm place for 1 hour, or until slightly spongy and bubby on top.

When the batter has finished resting, whisk the egg whites to soft peaks. Gently fold into the batter. Cover with clingfilm and set aside for a further 1 hour.

Heat a frying pan over a medium heat and brush with butter or oil. Add 4 tablespoons of the batter to the pan and cook for about 1 minute until bubbles form on top. Flip and cook for a further 30 seconds or so. Repeat until all the remaining batter is used up.

These are lovely served warm – they can be reheated in a 150°C/300°F/gas 2 oven for 5 minutes.

BUCKWHEAT

★

GALETTES

These slightly nutty, flavoursome crêpes are a specialty
in Brittany, where they're served a bit like sandwiches,
stuffed with all sorts of savoury goodies. Experiment with
fillings, but whatever you do, make sure there's cheese.

 MAKES 8 galettes

TAKES 40 minutes plus
1 hour 15 minutes resting
and returning to room
temperature

100g (3½oz/¾ cup) buckwheat
  flour
½ tsp sea salt flakes
1 egg
3 tbsp whole milk
1 tbsp melted butter
melted butter or vegetable oil,
  for frying

In a mixing bowl, whisk together the flour and
salt, and make a well in the centre. In a jug, whisk
together the egg, milk, melted butter, and 180ml
(6fl oz) cold water. Gradually pour the egg mixture
into the well and whisk, incorporating the flour as
you go, to make a smooth batter. Don't overbeat
or the galettes will be tough. Cover with clingfilm
(plastic wrap) and leave to rest in the fridge for
least 1 hour. Return the batter to room temperature
before cooking, adding a splash of water, if
necessary, to produce a batter the consistency of
single cream.

Heat a non-stick frying pan or crêpe pan over a
medium heat and brush with butter or oil. Pour
60ml (2fl oz/¼ cup) batter into the pan and quickly
swirl to cover the base. Cook for 1–2 minutes,
or until golden underneath. Flip and cook for a
further 30 seconds–1 minute. Repeat with the
remaining batter.

Serve the galettes immediately or layer them
between sheets of greaseproof paper and cover
loosely with foil to keep warm. Alternatively, keep
warm for a few minutes (any longer and they may
dry out) in a 100°C/225°F/¼ gas oven, layered
between sheets of greaseproof paper.

17

Pancake Basics

BUTTERMILK
★
PANCAKES

These fluffy beauties are tender within, golden without
and slightly crisp at the edges: joy. Not only heroes of the
breakfast table, they can also do a tasty savoury turn at
lunch and dinner. For many, they're the brightest stars in
the pancake firmament.

MAKES 10–12 pancakes

TAKES 30 minutes

150g (5oz/1¼ cups) plain
   (all-purpose) flour
1 tsp baking powder
½ tsp bicarbonate of soda
½ tsp sea salt
1 heaped tbsp caster (superfine)
   sugar
250ml (8½fl oz/1 cup) buttermilk
1 large egg, lightly beaten
1 tbsp melted butter
melted butter or vegetable oil,
   for frying

In a mixing bowl, whisk together the flour, baking
powder, bicarbonate of soda, salt, and sugar, and
make a well in the centre. In a jug, whisk together
the buttermilk, egg, and melted butter. Gradually
pour the egg mixture into the well and whisk,
incorporating the flour as you go, to make a
smooth batter. Don't overbeat or the pancakes will
be tough, though some small lumps are fine.

Heat a non-stick frying pan over a medium heat
and brush with melted butter or oil. Pour 60ml (2fl
oz/¼ cup) batter into the pan to make pancakes
roughly 10cm (4in) in diameter. Fry for 1–2 minutes,
or until bubbling on top and golden underneath.
You might need to adjust the heat to ensure
the pancakes don't overcook on the outside
before they are cooked through. Flip and cook
for 30 seconds–1 minute more. Repeat with the
remaining batter.

Serve straight from the pan or keep warm in a
150°C/300°F/gas 2 oven.

★

CRÊPES

This basic crêpe batter will form the basis of many a delicious feast. The batter will keep in the fridge for up to 24 hours. Alternatively, cook the crêpes, layer them between sheets of greaseproof paper, and freeze them in a plastic food bag for up to one month.

MAKES about 10 x 15-cm (6-in) crêpes

TAKES 50 minutes, plus 30 minutes resting

130g (4½oz/1 cup) plain (all-purpose) or wholemeal plain flour
1 tbsp caster (superfine) sugar (omit for savoury recipes)
½ tsp sea salt
1 egg, lightly beaten
300ml (10fl oz/1¼ cups) whole milk
1 tbsp butter, melted and cooled
melted butter or vegetable oil, for frying

In a mixing bowl, whisk together the flour, sugar, and salt, and make a well in the centre. In a jug, whisk together the egg, milk, and melted butter. Gradually pour the egg mixture into the well and whisk, incorporating the flour as you go, to make a smooth batter. Don't overbeat or the crêpes will be tough. Leave to stand for at least 30 minutes. The batter will thicken over this time, so stir in 1–2 tbsp cold water before cooking.

Heat a non-stick frying pan or crêpe pan over a medium heat and when hot enough – a sprinkle of water should hiss and sizzle – brush with butter or oil. Pour 60ml (2fl oz/¼ cup) batter into the pan, quickly swirling the pan to cover the base. Cook for 1–2 minutes until the edges of the crêpe look dry and the underneath is golden. Loosen the edges with a palette knife, flip, and cook for a further 1–2 minutes. Repeat with the remaining batter.

Serve the crêpes immediately or layer them between sheets of greaseproof paper and cover loosely with foil to keep warm. Alternatively, keep warm for a few minutes – any longer and they may dry out – in a 100°C/225°F/¼ oven, layered between sheets of greaseproof paper.

INDIAN

★

DOSAS

Dosas are fermented pancakes made from rice and lentil batter, and a staple in India, where they're wrapped around cooked vegetables, chutney, and other spiced fillings. There are various headache-inducing ways to make them, but this version is straightforward – just make sure the batter is not too thick.

 MAKES 8 x 15-cm
(6-in) dosas

 TAKES 1 hour, plus 12 hours
soaking and fermenting

50g (1¾oz) urid dal
½ tsp fenugreek seeds
150g (5oz/scant 1 cup) rice flour
1 tsp chilli oil
½ tsp sea salt flakes
vegetable oil, for brushing

Rinse the dal several times in cold water, then place it in a bowl with the fenugreek seeds. Cover generously with cold water and leave to soak for at least 4 hours, or overnight. Drain and rinse well, then transfer to a blender or food processor. Add 50ml (1¾fl oz) cold water and blitz until completely smooth.

Scrape into a mixing bowl, add the rice flour, oil, and salt, and stir in 300ml (10fl oz) cold water to make a thin batter. Cover with a clean tea towel and set aside to ferment for 8 hours.

Heat a non-stick frying pan over a medium heat and brush with oil. Pour 60ml (2fl oz/¼ cup) batter into the pan, swirling to cover the base. Lots of tiny bubbles should immediately form on top – if this doesn't happen, add a little more water to the batter. Cook for 1–2 minutes on each side.

Serve immediately or layer between sheets of greaseproof paper and cover loosely with foil to keep warm.

OATMEAL

PANCAKES

These might seem like temple food, but don't be deceived
by the healthy ingredients: they're delicious. The oats and
spelt give a lovely depth of flavour.

 MAKES 6 x 10-cm (4-in)
pancakes

 TAKES 30 minutes, plus
20 minutes resting

60g (2oz) rolled oats
180ml (6fl oz/¾ cup) whole milk
1 egg, lightly beaten
1 tbsp melted butter
90g (3oz/¾ cup) spelt flour
1 tsp baking powder
½ tsp ground cinnamon
1 tbsp light brown soft sugar
pinch salt
melted butter or vegetable oil,
    for frying

In a medium bowl, combine the oats and milk. Set
aside to rest for 20 minutes so the oats can soften,
then stir in the egg and melted butter.

In a large bowl, whisk together the flour, baking
powder, cinnamon, sugar, and salt, and make a
well in the centre. Gradually pour the oat mixture
into the well and whisk, incorporating the flour
as you go, to make a batter. Don't overbeat or
the pancakes will be tough. Add more milk, 1
tablespoonful at a time, if the batter seems too
thick – you want to achieve a soft dropping
consistency.

Heat a non-stick frying pan over a medium heat
and brush with butter or oil. Pour 60ml (2fl oz/
¼ cup) batter into the pan to make 10-cm (4-in)
pancakes. Cook for just over 1 minute, or until
bubbles form on top and the underneath is golden.
Flip and cook for 30 seconds –1 minute more.
Repeat with the remaining batter.

Serve straight from the pan or keep warm in a
150°C/300°F/gas 2 oven.

AUSTRALIAN
★
PIKELETS

Beware: these squidgy, fluffy numbers are quick, simple,
and intensely addictive. Gobble with jam and cream,
golden syrup, honey, or just cold salty butter.

 MAKES 16 pikelets

TAKES 25 minutes

150g (5oz/1¼ cups) self-raising
   flour
1 tsp baking powder
1 tbsp caster (superfine) sugar
generous pinch salt
1 egg, lightly beaten
180ml (6fl oz/¾ cup) whole milk
1 tbsp melted butter
vegetable oil, for brushing

In a mixing bowl, whisk together the flour, baking
powder, sugar, and salt, and make a well in the
centre. In a jug, whisk together the egg, milk, and
melted butter. Gradually pour the egg mixture into
the well and whisk, incorporating the flour as you
go, to make a smooth batter. Don't overbeat or the
pikelets will be tough.

Heat a frying pan over a medium heat and brush
with oil. Add tablespoonfuls of the batter and
cook for 1 minute, or until bubbles appear on
top. Flip and cook for a further 1 minute, or until
pale golden. Repeat until all the batter is used up.

Serve straight from the pan or keep warm in
a 150°C/300°F/gas 2 oven.

POTATO

★

PANCAKES

Serve these as an alternative to spuds with your favourite
meat or poultry dish. Alternatively, they're lovely adorned
with nothing but butter.

 MAKES 10 x 8-cm
(3-in) pancakes

 TAKES 30 minutes

400g (14oz) floury potatoes,
   peeled and cut into chunks
1 garlic clove, peeled and bruised
   with the side of a knife
   (optional)
1 tbsp butter
150ml (5fl oz/¾ cup) whole milk
½ tsp sea salt flakes
freshly ground black pepper
80g (3oz/scant ¾ cup) plain
   (all-purpose) flour
1 tsp baking powder
2 eggs, lightly beaten
small bunch chives, finely
   chopped (optional)
1 tbsp vegetable oil

Cook the potatoes and garlic (if using) in boiling
salted water until tender. Drain well, return the
potatoes and garlic to the pan and add the butter
and a splash of the milk. Mash until smooth and
creamy, and add salt and black pepper to taste.

Stir the flour and baking powder into the potatoes.
Gradually beat in the eggs until amalgamated, and
then enough of the milk to make a smooth, thick
batter. Stir in the chives (if using).

Heat a non-stick frying pan over a medium heat.
Add the oil and swirl to coat. Add large spoonfuls
of batter to the pan to make 8-cm (3-in) pancakes.
Cook for about 2 minutes, or until golden
underneath. Flip and cook for 1 minute more, or
until cooked through. Transfer to a 150°C/300°F/
gas 2 oven to keep warm while you repeat with the
remaining batter.

SOURDOUGH
★
PANCAKES

Tender, fluffy, and flavoursome, these pancakes are a
delicious way to use up unfed sourdough starter. For best
results, slather with butter and jam.

 MAKES about 12 pancakes

TAKES 15 minutes

250g (9oz) sourdough starter
1 egg
pinch salt
¼ tsp bicarbonate of soda
½ tsp baking powder
½ tbsp caster (superfine) sugar
1 tbsp vegetable oil, plus extra
 for frying

Stir all the ingredients together in a mixing bowl.

Heat a frying pan over a high heat and brush
with oil. Reduce the heat to medium, pour in
dessertspoonfuls of the batter (about 30ml/1fl oz)
and cook for 30 seconds–1 minute, or until bubbles
form on top and the underneath is golden. Flip and
cook for 30 seconds–1 minute more. Repeat with
the remaining batter.

Serve straight from the pan or keep warm in a
150°C/300°F/gas 2 oven.

VEGAN

★

PANCAKES

Flax seeds are incredibly nutritious, brimming with fibre, omega-3, and other good stuff. They are also eggcellent (!) egg replacers. If you can't find ready-ground seeds, grind whole ones in a spice mill or coffee grinder.

  MAKES about 8 pancakes

 TAKES 30 minutes, including 10 minutes thickening time

1 tbsp ground flax seeds (linseeds)
200ml (7fl oz/generous ¾ cup) almond milk
1 tbsp lemon juice
1 tbsp melted coconut oil, cooled, plus extra for frying
150g (5oz/1¼ cups) plain (all-purpose) white or wholemeal flour
1 heaped tbsp caster (superfine) sugar
1 tsp baking powder
½ tsp bicarbonate of soda
pinch salt
maple syrup or agave, to serve

In a small bowl, mix the flax seeds with 3 tbsp cold water and set aside for 10 minutes to thicken. Meanwhile, combine the almond milk, lemon juice, and coconut oil in a jug.

In a mixing bowl, whisk together the flour, sugar, baking powder, bicarbonate of soda, and salt, and make a well in the centre. Pour the soaked flax seeds into the well and then gradually stir in the milk mixture, incorporating the flour as you go, to produce a thick batter. You might not need all the milk. Be careful not to overstir; some small lumps are fine.

Heat a non-stick frying pan over a medium heat and brush generously with coconut oil. Pour 60ml (2fl oz/¼ cup) batter into the pan and cook until bubbles form on top and the underneath is golden. Flip and cook for a further 1 minute. Transfer to a 150°C/300°F/gas 2 oven to keep warm while you cook the remaining batter.

Serve warm, drizzled with maple syrup or agave.

BREAKFAST &

★

BRUNCH

ALMOND PANCAKES WITH
★
HONEY & BERRIES

These are light and fluffy, yet full of lovely almond flavour. They work a treat with the runny honey and crunchy seeds – you'll go nuts for them. Badum-tish!

MAKES 14 pancakes

TAKES 30 minutes

100g (3½oz/¾ cup) self-raising flour
100g (3½oz) ground almonds
1 tsp baking powder
2 tbsp dark brown soft sugar
2 eggs, separated
180ml (6fl oz/¾ cup) whole milk
melted butter or vegetable oil, for brushing
almond butter, runny honey, handful berries, and handful mixed seeds, to serve

In a mixing bowl, whisk together the flour, ground almonds, baking powder, and sugar, breaking up any lumps of sugar with the back of a spoon. Make a well in the centre. In a jug, whisk together the egg yolks and milk. Gradually pour the egg mixture into the well and whisk, incorporating the flour as you go, to make a smooth batter. Don't overbeat or the pancakes will be tough.

Whisk the egg whites to stiff peaks. Stir a large spoonful into the batter to loosen, then fold in the rest.

Heat a non-stick frying pan over a medium–low heat and brush generously with butter or oil. Drop 60ml (2fl oz/¼ cup) batter into the pan and cook for about 1 minute until bubbles just begin to form on top and the bottom is golden. These burn quite easily so cook them slowly and reduce the heat if necessary. Flip and cook for 30 seconds–1 minute more. Serve straight from the pan or keep warm in a 150°C/300°F/gas 2 oven while you cook the remaining batter.

To serve, stir the almond butter to loosen and spread some onto each pancake. Top with the berries, drizzle with honey, and scatter over some seeds.

CHEESE, EGG & SPINACH
★
BUCKWHEAT GALETTES

These tasty little pancake packets are very pleasing with their sunny egg yolks peeking through the top. If you make the batter the night before, you've got brunch for a small gathering pretty much in the can.

 MAKES 8 galettes

TAKES 1 hour 20 minutes, plus 1 hour 15 minutes resting and returning to room temperature for the batter

1 quantity Buckwheat galette batter (see page 17)

melted butter or vegetable oil, for frying
200g (7oz) Comté or Gruyère, grated
120g (4oz) baby spinach, chard or kale, very finely sliced
8 eggs

Heat a non-stick frying pan or crêpe pan over a medium heat and brush with butter or oil. Pour 60ml (2fl oz/¼ cup) batter into the pan and quickly swirl to coat the base. Cook for 1–2 minutes until golden underneath, then flip the galette and remove the pan from the heat.

Sprinkle one-eighth of the cheese in a circle on top of the galette, leaving enough room in the centre to hold an egg yolk. Top the cheese with one-eighth of the spinach, then crack an egg into the centre of the cheese-and-spinach circle. Return the pan to the heat and fold in the edges of the galette using a spatula to make a square. Cover – use a baking sheet if your frying pan doesn't have a lid – and cook for a few minutes until the egg white is firm and the yolk still runny.

Serve immediately. Repeat with the remaining batter and filling ingredients.

HONEYCOMB BUTTER

★

BUTTERMILK PANCAKES

Let's face it – honeycomb butter ain't no health food.
This might be an indulgent way to start the day, but a
glorious one for a special occasion.

 MAKES 16 pancakes

TAKES 2 hours, including
1 hour setting

For the honeycomb butter
vegetable oil, for brushing
100g (3½oz/scant ½ cup) caster
(superfine) sugar
2 tbsp golden syrup
2 tbsp runny honey
1 tsp bicarbonate of soda
250g (9oz) salted butter, softened

1 quantity Buttermilk pancake
batter (see page 18)
maple syrup, to serve

Line a rimmed baking sheet with baking paper. To make the honeycomb butter, combine the sugar, golden syrup, and 1 tablespoon of the honey in a pan and stir over a low heat, until the sugar dissolves. Simmer gently until the temperature reaches 150°C on a confectionary thermometer, or until a little dropped into a glass of cold water cracks and turns hard. Add the bicarbonate of soda, then remove the pan from the heat and whisk: the mixture will froth up dramatically. Quickly pour onto the prepared baking sheet and leave to harden for about 1 hour. Break half the honeycomb into pieces and place in a plastic food bag. Bash the bag with a rolling pin until the honeycomb is finely crushed but still coarse enough to give the butter some crunch.

Whip the butter and the remaining honey until light and fluffy, then fold in the crushed honeycomb. Spoon the butter onto a piece of clingfilm (plastic wrap), roll tightly into a sausage shape and chill. While this is happening, make the pancakes following the method on page 18, transferring them to a warm oven to keep warm.

Serve the pancakes warm with slices of the honeycomb butter on top and a generous drizzle of maple syrup.

EGGS & BACON WITH
★
SPRING ONION PANCAKES

Possibly the ideal breakfast for the morning after the
night before, these require just a little effort for rolling
– but are well worth it.

 MAKES 4 pancakes

TAKES 1 hour, including
30 minutes resting

For the pancakes
300g (10oz/2½ cups) plain
(all-purpose) flour, plus
extra for dusting
½ tsp sea salt flakes
about 300ml (10fl oz/1¼ cups)
freshly boiled water
toasted sesame oil, for brushing
60g (2oz) finely sliced spring
onions (scallions), white and
green parts
4 tbsp vegetable oil, for frying,
plus extra if needed

4 slices smoked back bacon
4 eggs
olive oil, for frying

Place the flour and salt in a mixing bowl and
gradually pour in the boiling water, stirring as you
go, to form a ball of sticky dough. Tip out onto
a lightly floured work surface and briefly knead
until smooth. Place in a bowl, cover with clingfilm
(plastic wrap), and set aside to rest for 30 minutes.

Divide the dough into four equal pieces and roll
into balls. Lightly dust a work surface with flour and
roll out one of the balls into a 25-cm (10-in) circle.
Keep the unused balls under a damp tea towel to
prevent them drying out. Brush generously with
sesame oil and scatter over one-quarter of the
spring onions. Roll into a sausage and then curl
around into a tight spiral. Roll out the snail into
a 20-cm (8-in) circle. Repeat with the remaining
dough balls.

Preheat the oven to 150°C/300°F/gas 2. Heat 1 tbsp
of the oil in a non-stick frying pan, add one of the
pancakes and cook for 2 minutes, pressing down
with an egg slice to flatten a little.

method continues overleaf...

★★★★★★★★★★★★★★★★

★ ★

EGGS & BACON WITH SPRING ONION PANCAKES
continued...

The pancake should be sizzling in oil, so if the pan looks a bit dry, add a splash more. When the pancake is golden underneath, flip and cook for a further minute. Transfer to the oven while you cook the remaining pancakes.

Heat a chargrill pan over a high heat, add the bacon and cook without moving until the fat turns golden. Turn over and cook until done to your liking. Keep warm in the oven with the pancakes. Using kitchen paper, wipe the pan used to cook the pancakes and fry the eggs in a little olive oil to your liking.

To serve, top a pancake with an egg and a bacon rasher and fold over.

COCONUT CRÊPES WITH
★
STRAWBERRY CHIA JAM

This quick-to-make jam goes beautifully with the pancakes, which taste gently of coconut and are ever so slightly chewy. This makes more jam than you need for one batch, but it keeps well an airtight jar in the fridge for a few days.

  MAKES 10 crêpes

TAKES 40 minutes, plus 30 minutes resting

For the jam
500g (1lb 2 oz) strawberries, hulled and quartered
2–3 tbsp runny honey, to taste
squeeze lemon juice
3 tbsp chia seeds, plus extra if needed

For the crêpes
3 tbsp desiccated coconut
130g (4½oz/1 cup) plain (all-purpose) white flour
3 tbsp coconut flour
2 tbsp caster (superfine) sugar
½ tsp sea salt
1 large egg, lightly beaten
200ml (7fl oz/generous ¾ cup) coconut milk
1 tbsp coconut oil, melted and cooled, plus extra for frying
Greek-style yoghurt, to serve

Start by making the jam. Place the strawberries in a pan and mash using a potato masher. Cook over a low–medium heat, stirring, until the berries release their juices. Stir in the honey and lemon juice, increase the heat, and simmer for 10 minutes, or until thickened. Remove from the heat and stir in the chia seeds. Set aside for at least 15 minutes to cool and thicken.

Meanwhile, make the crêpes. Toast the desiccated coconut in a dry frying pan, moving it about constantly with a wooden spoon, until pale gold. Transfer to a mixing bowl, then add the flours, sugar, and salt, and whisk to combine. Make a well in the centre. In a jug, whisk together the egg, coconut milk, 1 tbsp coconut oil, and 100ml (3½ fl oz/scant ½ cup) cold water. Gradually pour the egg mixture into the well and whisk, incorporating the flour as you go, to make a smooth batter. Don't overbeat or the crêpes will be tough. Set aside to rest for at least 30 minutes, then stir in 3 tablespoons of cold water to thin out a little.

method continued overleaf...

COCONUT CRÊPES WITH STRAWBERRY CHIA JAM

continued...

Heat a non-stick frying pan or crêpe pan over a medium–high heat and brush generously with coconut oil. Pour 60ml (2fl oz/¼ cup) batter into the pan, quickly swirling the pan as you go, to cover the base. Cook for 1–2 minutes until the top starts to look dry and the bottom golden. Flip and cook for a further 30 seconds and repeat with the remaining batter.

Serve the crêpes immediately or layer them between sheets of greaseproof paper and cover loosely with foil to keep warm. Alternatively, keep warm for a few minutes – any longer and they may dry out – in a 100°C/225°F/gas ¼ oven, layered between sheets of greaseproof paper.

To serve, spread each pancake with a tablespoon of the jam, roll up, then top with a little more jam and a splodge of yoghurt.

CORNMEAL PANCAKES
★
CHORIZO & TOMATO SALSA

Creamy polenta is turned into golden pancakes here,
served with a punchy salsa and nuggets of crispy chorizo.
It makes a hearty brunch.

SERVES 6

TAKES 1 hour

1 tbsp olive oil
150g (5oz) cooking chorizo,
    cut into small chunks
For the pancakes
200g (7oz/1⅓ cups) fine cornmeal
1 tsp sea salt flakes
400ml (14fl oz/1¾ cups)
    hot vegetable stock
1 egg, lightly beaten
300ml (10fl oz/1¼ cups)
    freshly boiled water
3 tbsp olive oil
For the salsa
2 avocados, peeled and chopped
250g (9oz) ripe tomatoes, finely
    chopped
½ red onion, finely chopped
1 large red chilli, seeded and
    finely sliced
1 tbsp lime juice, or more to taste
1 small bunch coriander (cilantro),
    chopped
Tabasco sauce, to taste

Heat the oil in a frying pan and fry the chorizo until
starting to crisp and the spicy oil has been released.
Transfer the chorizo and oil to a bowl and set aside.
Wipe out the pan using kitchen paper.

To make the pancakes, place the cornmeal, salt,
stock, and egg together in a pan and simmer over
a medium heat, stirring constantly for 4–5 minutes
until the mixture is very thick. Pull the pan off the
heat and stir in the freshly boiled water to make a
thick, smooth batter that will just drop off a spoon.

Heat a tablespoon of the oil in the frying pan used
to cook the chorizo. Drop in large spoonfuls of the
polenta mixture, spreading it out a little to make
8-cm (3-in) pancakes. Cook for 4–5 minutes on
each side until golden – don't try to turn them too
early or they won't hold together. Add more hot
water to the cornmeal batter as you go to maintain
the right consistency or it will become too thick.
Transfer the pancakes to a 150°C/300°F/gas 2 oven
to keep warm.

For the salsa, combine all the ingredients in a bowl.

Serve two pancakes per person, topped with the
chorizo and its oil, and the salsa.

FLUFFY BANANA
★
SULTANA PANCAKES

Bananas and sultanas are meant for each other, especially
when snuggled up together in a tender pancake.

 MAKES 8 pancakes

 TAKES 25 minutes

100g (3½oz/¾ cup) self-raising
  flour
½ tsp baking powder
pinch salt
1 tsp ground cinnamon
1 large ripe banana, mashed,
  plus sliced banana to serve
100ml (3½fl oz/scant ½ cup)
  whole milk
1 large egg
1 tbsp melted butter
40g (1¼oz) sultanas
melted butter or vegetable oil,
  for frying
runny honey or maple syrup,
  to serve

In a mixing bowl, whisk together the flour, baking
powder, salt, and cinnamon. In a jug, stir together
the mashed banana, milk, egg, and melted butter.
Gradually stir the wet ingredients into the dry until
well combined. Don't overbeat or the pancakes will
be tough, though some small lumps are fine. Stir in
the sultanas.

Heat a non-stick frying pan over a medium heat
and brush with butter or oil. Drop 60ml (2fl oz/
¼ cup) batter into the pan and cook for about
1 minute, or until golden underneath. Adjust the
heat as needed to ensure the pancakes don't burn
underneath before they are cooked through. Flip
and cook for a further 30 seconds–1 minute. Repeat
with rest of the batter. Serve straight from the pan
or keep warm in a 150°C/300°F/gas 2 oven while you
cook the remaining batter.

Serve the pancakes with slices of banana and a
drizzle of honey or maple syrup.

GRANOLA &
★
BLUEBERRY PANCAKES

These have a gorgeous flavour and some crunchy texture
from the granola: it's basically a selection of breakfast
dishes tumbled into one batch of tasty pancakes.

 MAKES 10–12 pancakes

 TAKES 30 minutes

1 quantity Buttermilk pancake
  batter (see page 18)

200g (7oz) Greek-style yoghurt
60g (2oz) strawberry jam, stirred
  to loosen
100g (3½oz) good-quality granola
100g (3½oz) blueberries, cut in
  half if very large
melted butter or vegetable oil,
  for brushing

Swirl the yoghurt and jam together in a bowl until
almost combined – it's nice to have some visible
trails of pink. Chill until needed.

Tip the granola into a zip-lock bag and lightly bash
with a rolling pin to break up any big clusters. Fold
into the pancake batter, along with the blueberries.

Heat a non-stick frying pan over a medium heat
and brush with butter or oil. Pour 60ml (2fl oz/
¼ cup) batter into the pan to make pancakes
roughly 10cm (4in) in diameter. Fry for 1–2 minutes,
or until bubbling on top and golden underneath.
Flip and cook for a further minute, pressing down
gently with an egg slice. Repeat until all the batter
is used up. Serve straight from the pan or keep
warm in a 150°C/300°F/gas 2 oven.

Serve warm, topped with the strawberry jam
yoghurt.

SRI LANKAN

★

HOPPERS

A hopper is a Sri Lankan breakfast pancake that's becoming increasingly popular in the US, the UK, and beyond. They're a bit fiddly to make at first but get easier with practice. Hopper pans are widely available from specialty food stores.

MAKES about 15 hoppers

TAKES about 1 hour, plus 2 hours resting

½ tsp fast-action dried yeast
100ml (3½fl oz/scant ½ cup) lukewarm water
250g (9oz/scant 1½ cups) rice flour
¼ tsp baking powder
pinch bicarbonate of soda
¼ tsp caster (superfine) sugar
pinch salt
300ml (10fl oz/1¼ cups) coconut milk, plus extra if needed
eggs, to serve (optional)

Dissolve the yeast in the lukewarm water. Sift the flour into a mixing bowl, add the baking powder, bicarbonate of soda, sugar, and salt, and mix well. Pour in the yeast mixture and the coconut milk, and stir to make a smooth batter. Cover and set aside to rest for 1–2 hours. Whisk well before cooking; the batter should be slightly watery and thinner than standard pancake batter, so add more coconut milk if needed.

Heat a non-stick hopper pan over a medium heat until smoking. Pour a ladleful of the batter into the centre of the pan and then swirl to coat the base and sides. If making an egg hopper, crack the egg into the centre now. Cover and cook for 3–5 minutes until the hopper is golden and the egg is cooked (if using). Loosen the edges using a palette knife and gently ease out onto a plate.

Serve immediately and repeat with the remaining batter.

LEMON

★

RICOTTA PANCAKES

This combo has quite rightly become a breakfast classic.
The cloud-like pancakes have a lovely lemony zing and
are awesome paired with plump, juicy berries. A drizzle of
honey and you're on your way to a very good day indeed.

 MAKES 8 pancakes

 TAKES 40 minutes

60g (2oz/½ cup) plain
   (all-purpose) flour
½ tsp baking powder
1½ tbsp caster (superfine) sugar
pinch sea salt
180g (6oz) ricotta
100ml (3½fl oz/scant ½ cup)
   whole milk
2 eggs, separated
melted butter or vegetable oil,
   for frying
runny honey and blueberries,
   to serve

In a mixing bowl, whisk together the flour, baking powder, sugar, and salt. In a jug, beat together the ricotta, milk, and egg yolks until smooth. Pour the egg mixture into the dry ingredients and stir to make a smooth batter.

Whisk the egg whites to stiff peaks. Stir a large spoonful into the batter to loosen, then fold in the rest.

Heat a non-stick frying pan over a medium heat and brush with melted butter or oil. Drop 60ml (2fl oz/¼ cup) batter into the pan and cook for 1–2 minutes until golden underneath. Flip and cook for a further minute. Serve straight from the pan or keep warm in a 150°C/300°F/gas 2 oven while you cook the remaining batter.

Serve warm drizzled with honey and blueberries on the side.

MOROCCAN PANCAKES

★

LEMON HONEY BUTTER

Spongy, yeasty, and full of holes to slurp up all that
honey butter, these are gorgeously like crumpets but
a lot easier to make.

 MAKES 14 pancakes

TAKES 55 minutes,
including proving
and frothing

For the batter
400ml (14fl oz/1¾ cups)
   whole milk
7g fast-action dried yeast
1 tbsp caster (superfine) sugar
140g (5oz/1¼ cups) fine
   semolina flour
60g (2oz/½ cup) plain
   (all-purpose) flour
½ tsp sea salt flakes
1 tsp baking powder
For the lemon honey butter
45g (1½oz) butter
60ml (2fl oz/¼ cup) honey
1 tbsp lemon juice, or to taste

Start by making the batter. Heat the milk in a small pan until lukewarm. Remove from the heat, stir in the yeast and sugar, and set aside for 5–10 minutes to froth.

In a mixing bowl, whisk together the flours, salt, and baking powder, then stir in the yeast mixture. Scrape into a blender and blitz until very smooth. Wipe out the mixing bowl using kitchen paper, pour the batter back in, then cover with clingfilm (plastic wrap). Set aside to prove for 30 minutes – the batter should have swelled in size with bubbles on top.

Meanwhile, make the lemon honey butter. Melt all the ingredients together in a small pan over a medium heat. Simmer for 30 seconds, then remove from the heat and set aside to keep warm.

Heat a non-stick frying pan over a low–medium heat. Stir the batter to deflate, then pour 60ml (2fl oz/¼ cup) batter into the pan. Cook for about 3 minutes until bubbles form and pop and the batter dries. Do not flip: adjust the heat as necessary so that the pancakes turn golden underneath without burning. Transfer to a plate and cover loosely with foil while you cook the remaining batter.

Serve the pancakes warm, with the lemon honey butter drizzled over.

OATMEAL PANCAKES

★

FRUIT SALAD & LIME SYRUP

If you're lucky enough to live in hot, sunny climes, griddle the fruit on the BBQ for an extra-smoky flavour. The most time-efficient way to prepare this is to griddle the fruit while the oats and milk in the pancake batter are resting.

 SERVES 4

 TAKES 50 minutes, plus
20 minutes resting

1 quantity Oatmeal pancake
  batter (see page 25)

3 tbsp butter
120ml (4fl oz/½ cup) maple syrup
juice and zest 1 lime
¼ pineapple, peeled, cored,
  and thickly sliced
2 peaches, peeled, stoned,
  and quartered
2 mangoes, peeled and thickly
  sliced
Greek-style yoghurt, to serve

Place the butter, maple syrup, and lime juice and zest in a small pan and melt together over a medium heat. Allow the syrup to bubble for 30 seconds or so to thicken a little, then remove from the heat and set aside to cool.

Place the fruit in a bowl, pour over the syrup and gently toss to coat. Heat a chargrill pan until hot, and add the fruit, shaking any excess syrup back into the bowl. Cook until lightly charred underneath, then turn and cook the other side – for about 5 minutes in total. Set the pan half-on, half-off a low heat to keep warm.

Pour the syrup left in the fruit bowl back into the small pan you cooked it in and warm through over a low heat.

Cook the pancakes following the method on page 25.

To assemble, serve two pancakes per person, top with one-quarter of the griddled fruit, and spoon over some of the syrup. A splodge of Greek-style yoghurt on top is highly recommended.

PANCAKES

★

EGGS BENEDICT

Pancakes make a perfect base for this classic breakfast dish, traditionally served with English muffins.

 MAKES 6 pancakes

 TAKES 1 hour

6 Buttermilk pancakes – ½ quantity Buttermilk pancake batter (see page 18)

6 eggs

6 thick ham slices

For the hollandaise

2 egg yolks

½ tsp white wine or tarragon vinegar

sea salt flakes

100g (3½oz) unsalted butter, melted

1 tsp lemon juice, or more to taste

Once you have made the pancakes, keep them warm in a 150°C/300°F/gas 2 oven and get on with the hollandaise.

Place the egg yolks, vinegar, and a pinch of salt in a heatproof bowl set over a pan of barely simmering water. Whisk continuously until pale and thick. Remove the bowl from the pan and very gradually whisk in the melted butter until completely incorporated and creamy. Add lemon juice to taste, then keep warm until needed.

To poach the eggs, crack 2 eggs into a cup. Fill a pan 5cm (2in) with water, bring to a simmer, and swirl with a spoon to make a whirlpool. When the whirlpool subsides, slide the eggs into the centre, increase the heat, and swirl the whites into place using a spoon. Reduce the heat to a bare simmer, then cook for 2–3 minutes, or until the whites are set and the yolks runny. Lift out with slotted spoon and drain on kitchen paper. Repeat with the remaining eggs.

Serve one pancake per person, topped with a slice of ham, a poached egg, and a generous spoonful of hollandaise.

★

NECTARINE & LIME COMPOTE

Mouth-puckering lime really brings out the flavour of
fragrant nectarines – it's a delectable combination that
might have you licking the compote pot.

  SERVES 4

TAKES 50 minutes, plus
30 minutes resting

1 quantity Crêpe batter, made
   with wholemeal flour
   (see page 20)
For the compote
6 nectarines, stoned and quartered
4 tbsp caster (superfine) sugar,
   plus extra to taste if needed
1 tsp ground ginger
zest and juice 2 limes, plus
   extra to taste if needed
2 tbsp butter
Greek-style yoghurt, to serve

While the crêpe batter is resting, make the
compote.

Place the nectarines in a bowl and toss with the
sugar, ginger, and lime zest. Heat the butter in a
frying pan and when foaming, add the nectarines
in a single layer, cut-side down. Fry over a medium–
high heat for about 5 minutes, turning the fruit
halfway through so both cut sides caramelize and
turn golden. Reduce the heat, add the lime juice
and a splash of water, and simmer until just cooked
through and the liquid has thickened into a syrup.
Have a taste: the syrup should be a lovely zingy
balance of sharp and sweet, so add more lime juice
or sugar as needed.

Cook the crêpes according to the method on
page 20, covering them loosely with foil as you
go to keep warm.

Fold the crêpes into quarters and serve two per
person, topped with the nectarine compote and
syrup, and a splodge of yoghurt.

LUNCH &

★

LIGHT BITES

BEETROOT BLINIS WITH
★
SMOKED MACKEREL & DILL

Gorgeously crimson, these make a fab starter or bite to have with drinks. Just a note: read this recipe through before you start making the blini batter, as you need to add the beetroot early on in the process.

MAKES 40 blinis

TAKES 1 hour,
plus 2 hours resting

For the blinis
200g (7oz) cooked beetroot,
   roughly chopped
1 quantity Blini batter
   (see page 14)

For the topping
250g (9oz) smoked mackerel fillets,
   skin removed
4 hard-boiled eggs, finely chopped
120g (4oz) crème fraîche
120g (4oz) cream cheese
small bunch dill, thick stalks
   removed, finely chopped,
   plus extra fronds to serve
freshly ground black pepper
lemon juice, to taste
3 tbsp finely chopped capers

To make the blinis, place the beetroot in a food processor and blitz to a smooth purée. Stir the purée into the blini batter when you first combine the wet and dry ingredients, as described on page 14.

While the blini batter is resting, get on with the topping. Flake the mackerel into a bowl, then add the eggs, crème fraîche, cream cheese, dill, and black pepper. Mash with a fork to make a well-combined but slightly rough mixture. Stir in lemon juice to taste. Set aside.

Cook the blinis following the method on page 14, transferring them to a 150°C/300°F/gas 2 oven to keep them warm.

To serve, top the warm blinis with a spoonful of the mackerel mixture, a dill frond, and a few chopped capers.

BLINIS WITH

★

CAMPARI-CURED SALMON

You need to start this celebratory dish a few days ahead
to give the salmon time to cure and absorb all the lovely
flavours, but it's very simple to prepare. This makes more
salmon than you will need for the blinis but there are
plenty of other uses for it – it's delicious draped over sliced
pumpernickel bread or folded through scrambled eggs.

 MAKES 40 blini

 TAKES 1 hour, plus 48–72
hours curing and resting

For the salmon
1 tbsp juniper berries
60g (2oz/¼ cup) caster (superfine)
  sugar
90g (3oz) sea salt flakes
finely grated zest 1 blood orange
  and juice ½ (standard oranges
  are fine)
½ tsp black peppercorns
1 tbsp Campari
8 drops Angostura bitters
2 bunches dill, roughly chopped
1 side of salmon in 2 halves, about
  1.2kg (2lb 10oz), skin on

1 quantity Blini batter (page 14)
crème fraiche and dill fronds,
  to serve

To make the salmon, toast the juniper berries in
a dry frying pan for a few minutes, until fragrant.
Transfer to a mortar, add the sugar, salt, orange
zest, and peppercorns, and pound to crush. Scrape
into a bowl and stir in the Campari, bitters, and
orange juice. Find a dish large enough to hold the
salmon and line with clingfilm (plastic wrap) so
that it overhangs the sides. Place one piece of
the salmon skin-side down in the dish and spread
the salt mixture on top. Cover with the dill, then
place the second piece of salmon on top, skin-side
up. Fold over the overhanging clingfilm to make a
sealed package. Place a small chopping board on
top and weigh down with food cans. Chill for 48–72
hours, turning the fish over every 12 hours. Pour off
any liquid in the dish.

Cook the blinis as instructed on page 14.

Just before serving, scrape the salt and dill off the
salmon and slice as thinly as possible. Serve the
blinis with curls of salmon on top, a spoonful of
crème fraiche, and a dill frond.

BUCKWHEAT GALETTES,
★
FIGS, GORGONZOLA & HONEY

The truffle honey is ambrosial here, but go lightly or it will overpower the other lovely flavours. Make the galettes ahead of time if you like, then all you have to do is prepare the filling and pop them under the grill.

 MAKES 8 galettes

 TAKES 1 hour, plus 1 hour 15 minutes resting and returning to room temperature

1 quantity Buckwheat galette batter (page 17)
2 tbsp butter, plus extra, melted, for frying and brushing
8 fresh figs, cut into quarters lengthways
240g (8½oz) Gorgonzola
80g (3oz) toasted walnuts, chopped
truffle honey, to serve (optional)

While the galette batter is returning to room temperature after resting, prepare the figs. Melt the butter in a frying pan and when foaming, add the figs, cut-side down. Cook for 1 minute or so, or until caramelised, then flip onto the other cut side and cook for a further minute. Transfer to a plate and set aside.

Cook the galettes following the method on page 17 – there's no need to keep them warm. Preheat the grill to high and line a baking sheet with baking paper.

Lay a galette flat on a chopping board and arrange four fig quarters on the bottom half. Break or cut one-eighth of the Gorgonzola into small pieces and dot them around the figs. Scatter over one-eighth of the walnuts. Fold the galette over into a half-moon shape and in half again to make a triangle. Transfer to the prepared baking sheet and brush the top with a little melted butter. Repeat with the remaining galettes and fillings.

Place the galettes-loaded baking sheet on the centre shelf under the grill for a few minutes until the Gorgonzola is oozy and bubbly. Serve hot, drizzled with truffle honey (if using) and a big green salad on the side.

TOMATO SALSA,

★

CORN & SPINACH PANCAKES

Sweet and juicy corn kernels really make these pancakes
pop with flavour. Kernels cut fresh from the cob are ideal,
but the canned stuff also works nicely.

 MAKES 8 pancakes

TAKES 30 minutes

For the salsa

3 ripe tomatoes, about 160g
   (5½oz), finely chopped
1 red onion, finely sliced
60g (2oz) feta, crumbled
1 tbsp lime juice, or more to taste
3 tbsp extra virgin olive oil
sea salt flakes
freshly ground black pepper

For the pancakes

160g (5½oz/1¼ cups) self-raising
   flour
1 tsp sea salt
1 tsp ground coriander
½ tsp ground cumin
1 tsp smoked paprika
1 egg, lightly beaten
1 tbsp olive oil, plus extra
   for frying
250g (9oz) corn kernels, from
   corn cobs or a can
60g (2oz) spinach, finely sliced

Make the salsa by combining all the ingredients in a
bowl. Set aside to allow the flavours to mingle.

For the pancakes, whisk together the flour, salt,
and spices. Stir in the egg and oil, and then 130ml
(4½fl oz/½ cup) cold water, or enough to make a
smooth batter. Fold in the corn and spinach – the
batter will be very thick.

Heat a frying pan over a high heat and brush with
oil. Reduce the heat to medium and pour 60ml (2fl
oz/¼ cup) batter into the pan. Use the back of a
spoon to flatten the batter into a patty shape and
cook for 2 minutes on each side, until golden and
cooked through. Repeat with the remaining batter.

Serve the pancakes hot, with a big spoonful of salsa
on the side. They are also delicious served with a
fried egg on top.

COURGETTE &
★
HALLOUMI PANCAKES

A bright and lovely light meal, these pancakes are
bursting with spring flavours. Enjoy them with a hefty
dose of sunshine if you can.

 MAKES 12 pancakes

TAKES 25 minutes

2 medium courgettes (zucchini)
   (about 500g/1lb 2oz)
1 tsp sea salt flakes
1 quantity Buttermilk pancake
   batter (page 18)
200g (7oz) halloumi, grated
handful basil leaves, torn
handful mint leaves, finely sliced
3 spring onions (scallions),
   finely sliced
grated zest 1 lemon
freshly ground black pepper
garlic-infused olive oil (plain
   olive oil is fine), for frying
pea shoots and lemon wedges,
   to serve

Grate the courgettes on the largest holes of a box
grater. Transfer to a sieve set over a bowl and toss
with the salt. Set aside for 15 minutes to drain,
then place in a clean tea towel and squeeze tightly
to remove as much liquid as possible. Loosen the
courgettes – they'll be tightly packed together –
then add to the pancake batter along with all the
remaining ingredients, except the oil, pea shoots,
and lemon wedges.

Heat a non-stick frying pan over a medium heat
and brush generously with the oil. Add large
spoonfuls of batter to the pan to make 10-cm
(4-in) pancakes and cook for 2 minutes until golden
underneath. Flip and cook for a further 2 minutes.

Serve the pancakes sprinkled with sea salt and
a handful of pea shoots, and lemon wedges on
the side.

ONION, APPLE,

★

BACON & COMTÉ CRÊPES

The combination of the nutty cheese, soft, sweet onion
and sharp apple is a French classic that makes a gorgeous
light lunch – it's kind of a pancake tart.

SERVES 4

TAKES 1 hour

3 tbsp olive oil, plus an extra
   splash
600g (1lb 5oz) onions, chopped
leaves from 1 thyme sprig
pinch sea salt flakes
2 garlic cloves, finely chopped
freshly ground black pepper
4 rashers smoked back bacon,
   chopped
1 crisp red apple
100g (3½oz) Comté, grated
   (Gruyère or even Cheddar
   would be fine)
4 crêpes – ½ quantity
   Crêpe batter (page 20)
1 tbsp melted butter

Line a baking sheet with baking paper and set the
grill to high.

Warm the oil in a large frying pan and add the
onions, thyme, and salt. Fry gently for about 15
minutes, until soft and starting to turn golden. Stir
in the garlic, season with black pepper and fry for
a couple of minutes more. Transfer to a bowl, then
wipe out the pan.

Return the pan to a medium–high heat, add a splash
of oil, and cook the bacon, until starting to crisp at
the edges. Pull the pan off the heat and pour out all
but 1 tablespoonful of the oil. Finely slice the apple,
then gently toss with the bacon over the heat.

Place a crêpe on the prepared baking sheet and
spoon one-quarter of the onion mixture into the
middle, leaving a 2-cm (¾-in) border. Top with one-
quarter of the bacon, apples, and Comté, pressing
down slightly to flatten just a little. Fold over the
crêpe border to make a square, pressing down to
keep it in place. Brush the folded edges with butter.
Repeat with the remaining crêpes. Place under the
grill and cook for 5 minutes, or until the cheese is
bubbling and the edges of the pancakes are crisp
and golden.

SAUTÉED MUSHROOMS WITH
★
DUTCH BABIES

A cross between muffins and Yorkshire puddings, these make wickedly tasty bites that are best served straight from the oven. Note: when you make the crêpe batter leave out the salt, as the lardons and cheese deliver loads of seasoning.

 MAKES 16 babies

TAKES 1 hour 20 minutes

2 tbsps (1½fl oz/scant ¼ cup) rapeseed or groundnut oil
1 quantity Crêpe batter (see page 20) – no need to rest
2 eggs, lightly beaten
splash olive oil
300g (10½oz) lardons
300g (10½oz) mixed mushrooms, chopped small
120g (4oz) grated Gruyère

Preheat the oven to 220°C/425°F/gas 7. Pour half a teaspoon rapeseed oil into each of the eight holes of a large, deep non-stick muffin tray – you will need to cook these babies in two batches. Place in the oven to heat up.

Meanwhile, pour the crêpe batter into a jug and beat in the eggs. Set aside.

Heat the olive oil in a frying pan and fry the lardons until crisp and golden at the edges. Transfer to a bowl using a slotted spoon. Add the mushrooms to the same frying pan and fry over a high heat, stirring, until tender and releasing their juices – don't be tempted to add more oil.

Have the grated Gruyère ready in a bowl. Working quickly, remove the muffin tray from the oven and distribute half the mushrooms, cheese, and bacon between the eight oiled holes. Fill each hole to around two-thirds with batter and return to the oven. Bake for 20–25 minutes – the babies should be puffed, golden, and just cooked through. Use a palette knife to ease them out onto a wire rack to cool a little. Add oil to the holes as before and repeat with the remaining fillings and batter. Serve hot.

ITALIAN

★

FARINATA

This giant chickpea pancake, known as *socca* in Provence,
is lip-smackingly lovely and redolent with rosemary. Slices
are best eaten warm straight from the pan, accompanied
by a glass of something cold.

 MAKES 1 large pancake

 TAKES 20 minutes, plus
30 minutes resting

125g (4½oz/1 cup) chickpea
(gram) flour
1 tsp sea salt flakes, plus extra
for sprinkling
2 tbsp finely chopped fresh
rosemary
75ml (2½fl oz) extra virgin olive
oil, plus extra for brushing

Combine the flour, salt, and rosemary in a mixing
bowl, then whisk in 2 tablespoons of the oil and
250ml (9fl oz/1 cup) cold water to make a smooth
batter, the consistency of double cream. Set aside
to rest for 30 minutes.

Meanwhile, preheat the oven to 200°C/400°F/gas 6.
Pour the remaining oil into a large ovenproof frying
pan and place in the oven to heat up.

When the batter has rested, quickly remove the
frying pan from the oven and pour the batter
into the hot oil, swirling to evenly cover the base.
Return to the oven and bake for about 10 minutes,
until firm and the edges are coming away from
the pan. Remove from the oven and set the grill
to high. Brush the top of the farinata with oil and
sprinkle with more salt. Grill for 3–5 minutes until
crisp and brown in patches on top. Serve warm,
in slices.

HAM HOCK &

★

ROSE HARISSA CRÊPES

Rose harissa in crêpe batter is a bit of a revelation,
imparting a lovely flavour and just a little heat. It tends
to be milder than some of the fiercer harissa pastes, so
take care if you use another variety.

 MAKES 6 crêpes

 TAKES 1 hour, plus 30
minutes standing

For the salad
1 avocado
60g (2oz) baby salad leaves
3 tbsp olive oil
1 tbsp lime juice
sea salt flakes
freshly ground black pepper
For the crêpes
1 tbsp rose harissa
1 quantity Crêpe batter (page 20)
vegetable oil, for brushing
180g (6½oz) ham hock, finely
  shredded
crème fraîche, to serve

Make the salad first so it's ready to serve as soon
as the crêpes are cooked. Peel, stone, and dice the
avocado, and place in a mixing bowl. Add the salad
leaves, oil, lime juice, and seasoning. Toss so the
leaves are nicely coated, then set aside.

Whisk the rose harissa into the crêpe batter. Heat a
non-stick frying pan or crêpe pan over a medium–
high heat and brush with oil. Pour a small ladleful of
the batter into the pan, swirling as you go to cover
the base. Before you set the pan back on the heat,
scatter one-sixth of the ham hock over the crêpe.
Return the pan to the stove and gently press the
ham hock into the crêpe with a spatula. Cook for
1–2 minutes, or until golden underneath. Carefully
flip the crêpe and cook for a further 30 seconds–
1 minute, pressing down with a spatula so the ham
hock takes on a bit of colour. Invert the crêpe onto
a plate so the ham hock faces up, and place a scoop
of the salad in the middle. Serve immediately,
with a spoonful of crème fraîche. Repeat with the
remaining crêpe batter and ingredients.

HAM, GRUYÈRE &
★
BÉCHAMEL CRÊPES

Children seem to fall on these like there's no tomorrow –
that's if they can get past the adults. There's something
about the cheesy, creamy savoury filling that makes
everyone a bit greedy.

SERVES 6

TAKES 1 hour 30 minutes,
plus 30 minutes resting

For the béchamel
250ml (9fl oz/1 cup) whole milk
¼ onion
1 bay leaf
20g (¾oz) butter
1 heaped tbsp plain (all-purpose)
   flour
pinch mustard powder (optional)
½ tsp sea salt flakes
grating nutmeg
freshly ground black pepper
100g (3½oz) grated Gruyère

1 quantity Crêpe batter
   (see page 20), rested
120g (4oz) good-quality ham,
   chopped or sliced

To make the béchamel, heat the milk, onion, and bay
leaf in pan, until steaming but not boiling. Remove
from the heat and discard the onion and bay leaf.
Melt the butter in a separate pan, add the flour, and
stir constantly for 1 minute over a medium heat until
well combined and bubbling. Remove the pan from
the heat and gradually whisk in the warm milk until
everything is amalgamated. Return the pan to the heat,
add the mustard powder (if using), salt, nutmeg, and
pepper. Simmer, stirring constantly, until thickened.
Reduce the heat to low, add the Gruyère, and stir until
melted and the sauce is smooth. Taste and add more
salt and black pepper if needed. Set the pan half-on,
half-off the low heat to keep warm while you get
on with the crêpes – but give the sauce a stir now
and then.

Make the crêpes following the method on page 20.
Transfer them to a plate stacked between sheets of
greaseproof paper, covered with foil, to keep warm.

To assemble, spread 3 tablespoons of the béchamel
over one half of a crêpe and top with one-sixth of the
ham. Fold the crêpe in half and then in half again to
make a triangle. Repeat with the remaining crêpes and
filling. Serve immediately, with a sharply dressed green
salad on the side.

KIMCHI

PANCAKES

Crunchy, chewy, and full of umami, these pancakes will
have you wanting more. If you like, you could make one
large sharing pancake instead of small ones.

 MAKES 6 pancakes

TAKES 25 minutes

For the pancakes
150g (5oz) kimchi
150g (5oz/1¼ cups) plain
 (all-purpose) flour
40g (1½oz/⅓ cup) cornflour
 (cornstarch)
2 spring onions (scallions),
 finely sliced
1 tsp sesame oil
generous pinch sea salt flakes
2 tbsp vegetable oil
For the dipping sauce
2 tbsp soy sauce
½ tsp sesame oil
1 tsp rice wine vinegar
splash yuzu or lime juice

Start by making the pancakes. Place the kimchi in a
sieve set over a mixing bowl and press down with
the back of a spoon to squeeze out the pickling
juices. Transfer the kimchi to a chopping board,
roughly chop, then return to the bowl with the
juices. Add all the remaining pancake ingredients,
except the vegetable oil. Gradually stir in 150ml
(5fl oz/generous ½ cup) cold water, or more if
needed, to make a thick batter. Set aside.

Combine all the dipping sauce ingredients in a small
bowl and set aside.

Heat a frying pan over a medium–high heat and
add 1 tablespoon of the vegetable oil, swirling
to coat the pan. When the pan is very hot, pour
60ml (2fl oz/¼ cup) batter into the pan and flatten
slightly to make a pancake. Fry for about 3 minutes,
or until the bottom of the pancake is crisp and
burnished. Flip, press down with a spatula, and fry
for a further 2 minutes. Repeat with the remaining
batter, adding more oil to the pan if needed. Serve
hot, with the dipping sauce alongside.

MASALA

★

DOSAS

These fermented pancakes are stuffed with a comforting, mildly spiced potato curry, made sweet with coconut milk.

 MAKES 8–10 dosas

 TAKES 1 hour 45 minutes, plus 12 hours soaking and fermenting

1 quantity Dosa batter (page 22)

For the potatoe curry
3 tbsp vegetable oil
1½ tsp mustard seeds
1 tsp cumin seeds
1 onion, chopped
3 small green chillies, finely sliced
pinch sea salt flakes
2 garlic cloves, finely chopped
1 tsp ground turmeric
1 heaped tsp garam masala
700g (1lb 9oz) potatoes, cut into 2-cm (¾-in) cubes
1 small tomato, chopped
½ tsp sea salt flakes, plus more to taste
160ml (5½fl oz/¾ cup) coconut milk
handful coriander (cilantro) leaves, chopped

Heat the oil in a frying pan over a medium–high heat until shimmering hot. Add the mustard and cumin seeds, moving them about in the oil with a wooden spoon. When the mustard seeds start to pop, reduce the heat to medium and add the onion, chillies, and salt. Gently fry for about 8 minutes until soft, turning the heat down if needed to avoid burning. Stir in the garlic, turmeric, and garam masala, and cook for a further 2 minutes. Add the potatoes and tomato, mixing to coat in the spiced oil. Pour in 100ml (3½fl oz/scant ½ cup) cold water and cook over a medium heat for 25–30 minutes, or until the potatoes are tender. You will need to add frequent splashes of water to keep the potatoes moist and prevent them sticking, but you don't want any liquid left at the end of cooking. When done, add the coconut milk and cook for a couple of minutes more. Finally, stir in the coriander.

Cook the dosas following the method on page 22, keeping them warm while you use up all the batter.

Place spoonfuls of the potato mixture in the centre of each dosa and roll into a cone shape. Serve immediately.

MEXICAN PANCAKES WITH
★
SMOKY CORN SALAD

Masa harina is an authentic Mexican flour made from corn kernels that are soaked in lime water before being finely ground. It makes delicious pancakes, here stuffed with oozy cheese and juicy kernels of corn.

MAKES 8 pancakes

TAKES 45 minutes

For the pancakes
100g (3½oz) masa harina
50g (2oz/scant ½ cup) self-raising flour
½ tsp baking powder
1 tsp sea salt flakes
1 tsp smoked paprika
100g (3½oz) queso fresco cheese (or feta) cut into small cubes
1 corn cob, kernels sliced off
2 tbsp vegetable oil
For the salad
2 corn cobs
olive oil, for brushing
2 large handfuls mint leaves, torn
2 large handfuls parsley leaves, torn
2 large handfuls coriander (cilantro) leaves, torn
1 bunch spring onions (scallions), finely sliced
60ml (2fl oz/¼ cup) lime juice
90ml (3fl oz/⅓ cup) olive oil
sea salt flakes
freshly ground black pepper

Start with the corn for the salad. Heat a chargrill pan until very hot and brush the two corn cobs with oil. Cook for about 10 minutes, turning frequently, until tender and charred. When cool enough to handle, slice off the kernels using a sharp knife, place in a salad bowl, and leave to cool.

Meanwhile, make the pancakes. Whisk together the masa harina, flour, baking powder, salt, and paprika. Gradually stir in 250ml (9fl oz/1 cup) cold water to make a thick batter. Fold in the cheese and the uncooked corn kernels.

Heat 1 tablespoon of the oil in a large frying pan and add large spoonfuls of the batter, flatting them into patties. Fry over a medium–high heat for about 4 minutes on each side, until golden and cooked through. Transfer to a plate in a 150°C/300°F/gas 2 oven as you go while you cook the rest of the batter, adding the remaining oil to the frying pan to cook the second batch.

To serve, add the remaining salad ingredients to the salad bowl and toss to coat. Serve two pancakes per person, topped with a generous scoop of the salad.

JAPANESE

★

OKONOMIYAKI

The name of these Japanese pancakes is derived from the word *okonomi* (meaning 'what you like') and *yaki* (meaning 'cooked'). Go the extra mile, if you can, to find bonito flakes – wisps of dried, smoked tuna that pack an extra umami punch.

 MAKES 4 okonomiyaki

 TAKES 55 minutes, plus 1 hour resting

240g (8½oz/2 cups) plain (all-purpose) flour
2 tsp baking powder
400ml (14fl oz/1¾ cups) cold dashi or vegetable stock
4 eggs, lightly beaten
50g (2oz) grated raw potato
2 tbsp tomato ketchup
2 tbsp Worcestershire sauce
1 tsp runny honey, or more to taste
1 tbsp soft white breadcrumbs
100g (3½oz) shredded cabbage
2 tbsp pickled ginger, finely chopped
sea salt flakes
freshly ground black pepper
4 tbsp vegetable oil
300g (10½oz) pork loin, sliced wafer-thin
Japanese mayonnaise
2 spring onions (scallions), finely sliced
bonito flakes (optional)

In a mixing bowl, whisk together the flour and baking powder. Gradually whisk in the dashi or stock to make a smooth batter. Stir in the eggs and potato. Transfer to the fridge to rest for 1 hour. Meanwhile, mix together the ketchup, Worcestershire sauce, and honey in a small bowl. Set aside.

When the batter has rested, mix in the breadcrumbs, cabbage, ginger, and salt and black pepper. Heat 1 tablespoon of the oil in a frying pan with a 15-cm (6-in) base and ladle in one-quarter of the batter. Swirl to coat the base. Arrange one-quarter of the pork on top of the pancake, cover, and cook for 3 minutes, or until the edges of the pancake turn brown. Flip, cover with a lid, and cook for 2–3 minutes more.

Slide the pancake onto a plate. Drizzle over some of the prepared sauce and the mayonnaise. Sprinkle with the spring onions and bonito flakes (if using). Serve immediately. Repeat with the remaining batter and ingredients.

PUDLA WITH
★
COCONUT CHUTNEY

These Indian crêpes are delicious and also good for you,
containing nothing more than chickpeas, vegetables,
garlic, and herbs. Halo alert.

 MAKES 8 pudla

 TAKES 1 hour 15 minutes,
plus 1 hour resting

For the pancakes
150g (5oz/1½ cups) chickpea
   (gram) flour
3 tbsp chopped coriander (cilantro)
1 green chilli, finely chopped
1 tsp cumin seeds
1 tsp sea salt flakes
1 tsp vegetable oil, plus extra
   for frying
large handful grated vegetables
   e.g. carrots, courgettes (zucchini),
   or spring onions (scallions)

For the chutney
80g (3oz) desiccated coconut
2 large handfuls coriander
   (cilantro) leaves and thin stalks
2 large handfuls mint leaves
8 medium green chillies
8 garlic cloves
2 tsp cumin seeds
120ml (4fl oz/½ cup) coconut
   milk, plus extra if needed
2 tsp caster (superfine) sugar
60ml (2fl oz/¼ cup) lime juice,
   plus more to taste
sea salt flakes, to taste

Start by making the pancakes. In a mixing bowl, whisk
together the chickpea flour, coriander, chilli, cumin
seeds, and salt. Gradually stir in the oil along with about
250ml (9fl oz/1 cup) cold water to make a batter the
consistency of single cream. Set aside to rest for 1 hour.

Meanwhile, make the chutney. Soak the coconut
in 150ml (5fl oz/generous ½ cup) cold water for 30
minutes, then drain and squeeze out the excess liquid.
Transfer to a blender or food processor, add all the
remaining chutney ingredients, and blitz until well
combined into a creamy mixture that retains some
texture. Taste and add more lime juice or salt if needed,
or more coconut milk if the chutney is too thick.
Transfer to a bowl and set aside.

Stir the vegetables into the pancake batter. Heat
a frying pan over a high heat and brush generously
with oil. Pour 60ml (2fl oz/¼ cup) batter into the pan,
swirling to coat the base. Reduce the heat to medium–
high and cook for 3–4 minutes until bubbles start to
form and the top begins to look dry. Loosen the edges
with a spatula, flip, and cook for 1–2 minutes. Transfer
to a plate, cover loosely with foil, and repeat with the
remaining batter.

Serve the pudla hot with the chutney alongside for
dunking, or wrapped inside, if you prefer.

RYE CRÊPES WITH

★

GOAT'S CHEESE & LARDONS

Rye flour is nutty and flavoursome, and makes these pancakes especially hearty. Paired with the vibrant salad, this is a substantial and pretty special lunch.

MAKES 6 crêpes

TAKES 50 minutes, including 30 minutes resting

For the crêpes
50g (2oz/scant ½ cup) plain (all-purpose) flour
50g (2oz/½ cup) rye flour
½ tsp sea salt
1 egg, lightly beaten
200ml (7fl oz/generous ¾ cup) whole milk
1 tbsp melted butter
olive oil, for frying

For the salad
100g (3½oz) smoked lardons
80g (3oz) baby salad leaves
180g (6½oz) soft goat's cheese, crumbled
½ red onion, finely sliced
small handful mint leaves

For the dressing
90ml (3fl oz/⅓ cup) extra virgin olive oil
2 tbsp lemon juice
sea salt flakes
freshly ground black pepper

Start by making the crêpe batter. Whisk the flours and salt in a mixing bowl and make a well in the centre. In a jug, whisk up the egg, milk, and melted butter. Gradually pour the egg mixture into the well and whisk, incorporating the flour as you go, to make a smooth batter. Don't overbeat. Leave to rest for 30 minutes.

Meanwhile, fry the lardons in a dry frying pan until crisp at the edges, then set the pan half-on, half-off a very low heat to keep warm. Combine the remaining salad ingredients in a salad bowl. Place all the dressing ingredients in a screw-top jar and shake to combine.

For the crêpes, stir the batter and add a few tablespoons of cold water if it is too thick – it should be the consistency of double cream. Heat a non-stick frying pan or crêpe pan and brush with oil. Add a small ladleful of the batter, swirling the pan as you pour so the base is thinly coated. Cook for 1 minute, or until golden underneath, then flip and cook for a further minute. Layer the crêpes between sheets of greaseproof paper and cover loosely to keep warm.

Add the lardons to the salad and toss with enough of the dressing to coat. Distribute the salad between the pancakes and fold in half. Serve immediately.

SMOKED SALMON &

★

CREAM CHEESE ROTOLLOS

Leftover pancakes – if there is such a thing in your house –
are terrific for rolling up tasty goodies: smoked salmon,
cream cheese, and cucumber are perfect partners.

 MAKES 12 slices

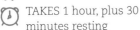 TAKES 1 hour, plus 30
minutes resting

4 leftover crêpes (or ½ quantity
   Crêpe batter on page 20)

140g (5oz) cream cheese
280g (10oz) smoked salmon,
   thinly sliced
160g (5½oz) cucumber, thinly
   sliced, ideally on a mandoline
1 bunch dill, fronds removed
handful cress
½ lemon
freshly ground black pepper

If you don't have any leftover crêpes, start by
making the batter and cooking 4 crêpes, then
leaving them to cool.

Place two crêpes side by side on a large piece of
clingfilm (plastic wrap), overlapping slightly. Spread
half the cream cheese all over the crêpes. Top
with half the smoked salmon, leaving a 1-cm (¾-in)
border on one of the shorter sides. Top with half
the cucumber, dill, and cress. Squeeze over a little
lemon juice and grind over some black pepper.

Starting from the end without the border, roll the
crêpes up tightly into a sausage shape, using the
clingfilm to help you. Gently press the edge down
to seal – the cream cheese will act like glue. Trim
the ends, then cut into 2-cm (¾-in) slices. Repeat
the process with the other two crêpes. Serve
immediately.

PANCAKE

★

DINNERS

PORK, FENNEL & CHILLI
★
BAKED PANCAKES

This is rib-sticking stuff, perfect served on a cold day.

SERVES 4

TAKES 1 hour

butter, for greasing
1 tbsp olive oil
500g (1lb 2 oz) minced (ground) pork
1 onion, finely chopped
1 garlic clove, finely chopped
2 tsp fennel seeds
½–1 tsp chilli flakes, according to taste
100ml (3½fl oz/scant ½ cup) red wine
1 tbsp tomato purée
500g (1lb 2oz) passata
salt and freshly ground black pepper
120ml (4fl oz/½ cup) double cream
10 crêpes – 1 quantity Crêpe batter (page 20)
1 mozzarella ball, grated
80g (3oz) Comté or Gruyère, grated
30g (1oz) grated Parmesan

Preheat the oven to 180°C/350°F/gas 4 and butter an 18x28-cm (7x11-in) or similar baking dish.

Heat the oil in a frying pan, add the pork, and break up with a spoon. Fry over a medium–high heat until browned; give it time to colour and get a little crispy. Transfer to a bowl with a slotted spoon. Tip out all but 2 tablespoons of the fat from the pan. Over a medium heat, stir the onion into the fat and cook for 6 minutes. Add the garlic, fennel seeds, and chilli flakes, and fry, stirring for 1–2 minutes, until you can smell the fennel.

Return the minced pork to the pan and stir until well combined with the onion. Add the wine and cook until it bubbles up and reduces, then stir in the tomato purée and passata. Season generously with salt and black pepper. Simmer gently, stirring now and then, for 20 minutes until the sauce has thickened. Remove from the heat and stir in the cream. Taste for seasoning and add more salt and black pepper if necessary.

Assemble, by spooning a generous amount of the ragu along the centre of each crêpe and neatly roll up. Place in the prepared dish, tucking the ends under. Repeat until you have five pancakes in the base. Scatter over half the mozzarella and Comté. Repeat with a second layer, finishing with the remaining mozzarella and Comté. Sprinkle the Parmesan over and bake for 25 minutes, or until golden. Serve hot, with a green salad.

CREAMED GREENS WITH
★
CHEESY PANCAKES

Wrapped around creamed greens these cheesey golden
pancakes make a delicious and healthy-ish supper.

MAKES 8 pancakes
(serves 4)

TAKES 1 hour, plus
30 minutes resting

For the pancakes
60g (2oz/½ cup) plain (all-purpose)
   flour
70g (2½oz) grated cheese such
   as Cheddar, Comté or Gruyère
½ tsp nigella seeds
pinch salt
2 eggs, lightly beaten
about 100ml (3½fl oz/scant ½ cup)
   whole milk
melted butter or vegetable oil,
   for frying

For the creamed greens
2 tbsp olive oil
3 tbsp butter
1 onion, very finely chopped
sea salt flakes and freshly ground
   black pepper
4 garlic cloves, finely chopped
400g (14oz) mixed greens such as
   kale, chard, and spinach, sliced
   and tough stalks discarded
1 tbsp finely grated lemon zest
150ml (5fl oz/¾ cup) double cream

Start by making the pancakes. In a mixing bowl, stir
together the flour, cheese, nigella seeds, and salt, and
make a well in the centre. In a jug, whisk together the
eggs and milk. Gradually pour the egg mixture into the
well and whisk, incorporating the flour as you go, to
make a smooth batter. Don't overbeat. Leave to stand
for at least 30 minutes while you make the greens.

For the greens, heat the oil and half the butter in a
frying pan over a medium heat until foaming. Reduce
the heat, then add the onion and a pinch of salt.
Gently fry for 5 minutes, or until very soft. Add the
garlic and cook for 2 minutes. Remove from the heat.

Cook the greens in boiling salted water for 2 minutes
until tender. Drain and squeeze out any excess liquid.
Return the onion pan to the heat and add the greens
and the remaining butter. Cook over a medium heat
to warm through. Stir in the cream and simmer until
thickened a little. Season to taste. Set aside.

Heat a non-stick frying pan over a medium heat and
brush with butter or oil. Pour 60ml (2fl oz/¼ cup)
batter into the pan and swirl to coat the base. Cook
for 2–3 minutes, or until golden underneath. Flip and
cook for 2 minutes. Remove to a plate and cover with
foil while you cook the remaining batter.

To serve, distribute the creamed greens between the
pancakes, roll up, and serve immediately.

CHESTNUT CRÊPES WITH
★
CREAMY MUSHROOMS

The crème fraîche and tarragon in this are terrific foils to
the subtle chestnut sweetness of the crêpes.

 MAKES 4 x 15-cm
(6-in) crêpes

 TAKES 30 minutes

For the crepes
80g (3oz/¾ cup) chestnut flour
pinch salt
½ tbsp extra virgin olive oil
melted butter or vegetable oil,
  for brushing
For the mushrooms
½ tbsp butter
½ tbsp olive oil
2 shallots, finely chopped
salt and freshly ground black
  pepper
300g (10oz) mixed mushrooms,
  such as button, oyster, and
  portobello, roughly chopped
2 garlic cloves, finely chopped
4 tbsp crème fraîche
2 tbsp finely chopped tarragon,
  plus extra for sprinkling
lemon juice, to taste
watercress, to serve

To make the crêpes, sieve the flour into a mixing bowl
and add the salt. Gradually stir in 150ml (5fl oz/generous
½ cup) cold water and the oil to make a smooth batter
the consistency of single cream. Set aside.

For the mushrooms, melt the butter and oil together in
a frying pan over a medium heat, add the shallots and a
pinch of salt, and fry until soft. Add the mushrooms and
garlic, and increase the heat to high; using a wooden
spoon, keep the mushrooms moving, scraping the
bottom of the pan, so nothing catches or burns. Cook
until the mushrooms are tender and releasing their
juices. Pull the pan off the heat and stir in the crème
fraîche and tarragon. Add lemon juice to taste, lots of
black pepper, and more salt if needed. Cover and set
the pan half-on, half-off a very low heat to keep warm.

Heat a non-stick frying pan or crêpe pan over a
medium–high heat and brush generously with butter
or oil. Pour a small ladleful of batter into the pan and
quickly swirl to coat – adjust the heat as needed to
prevent burning. When the crêpe begins to look dry on
top, loosen the edges using a palette knife and, when
golden underneath, flip. Cook for a further 30 seconds.
Transfer to a plate and cover loosely with foil to keep
warm while you repeat with the remaining batter.

Divide the mushrooms between the crêpes and roll up.
Sprinkle with tarragon and serve with watercress.

CHICKEN &

★

SWEETCORN PANCAKES

There's something about the combination of chicken, leek
and sweetcorn that's catnip for children – and adults will
shovel these down too.

 SERVES 6

 TAKES 45 minutes,
plus 30 minutes resting
for the batter

1 quantity Crêpe batter (page 20)
2 tbsp butter
3 leeks, finely sliced
6 chicken thighs, cut into thin
    strips
good glug white wine
sea salt flakes
freshly ground black pepper
150g (5oz) sweetcorn kernels
180g (6oz) Cheddar, grated

Melt the butter in a frying pan set over a medium
heat and add the leeks and chicken. Fry, stirring
frequently, until the leeks are soft and the chicken
is cooked through and starting to colour. Add the
wine, scraping the bottom of the pan as it bubbles
up and reduces. Season generously with salt and
black pepper, then set aside.

Preheat the grill to high and set the oven rack
about 10cm (4in) from the grill. Heat a non-stick
ovenproof frying pan or crêpe pan over a medium–
high heat and pour in a small ladleful of the batter,
swirling to coat the base. Cook for about 30
seconds, then top with one-sixth of the chicken
and leek mixture, and one-sixth of the corn. Cook
for a couple of minutes until golden and cooked
underneath, then remove from the heat. Scatter
over one-sixth of the cheese and place under the
grill for a further 2 minutes until the cheese is
bubbling. Serve immediately and repeat with the
remaining batter and toppings.

CHICKEN, CHILLI & BASIL

★

PANCAKE WRAPS

These are bit like Southeast Asian fajitas and are dang tasty.
If you like, bring the components to the table – pancakes,
chicken, and garnishes – and invite everyone to assemble
the wraps themselves. Don't forget the squeeze of lime –
it brings all the flavours to life.

 SERVES 4–6

 TAKES 1 hour 15 minutes

1 quantity Crêpe batter (page 20)
1 tsp chicken or vegetable stock
  powder
sesame oil, for brushing
For the chicken
4 garlic cloves, finely chopped
20g (¾oz) roughly chopped
  red chillies
generous pinch sea salt
2 tbsp vegetable oil
500g (1lb 2oz) chicken breast fillets
2 tbsp fish sauce
1 tbsp soy sauce
1 tbsp caster (superfine) sugar
large handful basil leaves, torn
To serve
135g (5oz) cucumber, cut into sticks
40g (1¼oz) coriander (cilantro)
  leaves
1 large red chilli, halved, deseeded
  and finely sliced lengthways
lime wedges

Whisk the stock powder into the crêpe batter
until dissolved, then make the crêpes following the
method on page 20 – there's no need to leave the
batter to rest for 30 minutes. Set aside.

Cut the chicken into thin strips. Pound the garlic,
chillies, and salt in a mortar to make a paste. Heat
the oil in a frying pan or wok, add the paste, and
stir-fry over a high heat for 30 seconds – be careful
not to burn the garlic. Add the chicken strips and
stir-fry for 2 minutes until just cooked through.
Add the fish sauce, soy sauce, and sugar, and stir-fry
for a further 30 seconds. Set aside to keep warm.

Set a chargrill pan over a high heat. While the pan
is heating, lightly brush one side of each crêpes
with sesame oil. Place a crêpe in the pan, oiled-side
down, and cook for 1 minute, or until charred with
stripes underneath. Flip and cook for 30 seconds
more. Transfer to a plate and repeat with the
remaining crêpes.

Place some of the chicken mixture on one half
of a crêpe. Top with some cucumber, coriander,
chilli, and a squeeze of lime juice. Roll up and scoff
immediately.

SQUASH & HERB YOGHURT
★
CHICKPEA CRÊPES

Sweet, crisp, and golden roasted squash is delicious here
partnered with hearty chickpea-flour crêpes.

 SERVES 4

 TAKES 1½ hours, including
resting time

For the pancakes
100g (3½oz/¾ cup) chickpea
 (gram) flour
1 tbsp garlic oil
½ tsp sea salt flakes
vegetable oil, for frying

For the yoghurt
300g (10oz) Greek-style yoghurt
4 heaped tbsp chopped fresh
 herbs such as basil, parsley,
 and chives
2 garlic cloves, crushed
1 tbsp extra virgin olive oil
½ tsp chilli flakes
zest 1 lime, plus lime juice to taste

For the squash
600g (1lb 5oz) butternut squash,
 peeled and chopped into 2-cm
 (¾-in) cubes
1 tbsp butter
1 tbsp olive oil
1 tbsp finely chopped rosemary
sea salt flakes
handful rocket (arugula), to serve

Start by making the pancakes. Whisk all the
ingredients together, except the vegetable oil, and
stir in 150ml (5fl oz/generous ½ cup) cold water to
make a smooth batter. Set aside for 1 hour.

Meanwhile, stir all the yoghurt ingredients together
in a bowl. Cover with clingfilm (plastic wrap) and chill.

Preheat the oven to 200°C/400°F/gas 6 and spread
the squash cubes in a single layer in a baking tray.
Melt the butter, oil, and rosemary together in a pan.
Pour the buttery oil over the squash, toss to coat,
and sprinkle with salt. Roast for 25–30 minutes,
turning the squash halfway through, until tender and
golden. Set aside and keep warm.

To cook the crêpes, heat a non-stick frying pan over
a high heat and brush with oil. Reduce the heat to
medium and pour 60ml (2fl oz/¼ cup) batter into
the pan, quickly swirling to cover the base. Cook for
30 seconds–1 minute, until the top begins to look
dry, then flip and cook for 10 seconds more. The
crêpes will barely take on any colour. Transfer to a
plate and cover loosely with foil to keep warm while
you repeat with the remaining batter.

To assemble, divide the squash and rocket between
the crêpes and generously spoon over some yoghurt.
Fold the pancakes over and serve immediately.

HOISIN SAUCE WITH
★
CHINESE DUCK PANCAKES

A tasty and sticky assemble-yourself dinner like this is
always a winner.

 SERVES 6

 TAKES 1 hour 25 minutes

For the marinade
6 duck legs
1 tbsp sea salt flakes
1 tbsp Chinese five spice
vegetable oil, for frying

For the pancakes
150g (5½oz/1¼ cups) plain
   (all-purpose) flour, plus
   extra for dusting
pinch salt
175ml (6fl oz/¾ cup) freshly
   boiled water
sesame oil, for brushing

To serve
1 large cucumber, deseeded
   and cut into thin sticks
2 bunches spring onions
   (scallions), finely sliced
   lengthways
hoisin sauce

Preheat the oven to 170°C/325°F/gas 3. Prick the
duck legs all over with a skewer and pat dry with
kitchen paper. Rub the salt and Chinese five spice
into the legs all over. Heat a splash of oil in a frying
pan and cook the legs, skin-side down over a high
heat, for about 6 minutes until the skin starts to
crisp and lots of fat is released. Be careful not to
burn the spice. Turn the legs over and brown the
other side.

Arrange the legs in a single layer in a baking tray and
roast for 1 hour–1 hour 15 minutes, or until you can
pull the meat away from the bones easily.

While the duck is cooking, make the pancakes.
Place the flour and salt in a bowl and gradually stir
in the freshly boiled water to make a shaggy dough.
Tip out onto a lightly floured work surface and
knead for 10 minutes to make a smooth, pliable
dough. Place in a covered bowl for 30 minutes.

Roll the dough into a sausage shape and cut into
12 equal pieces. Cut a piece of baking paper into a
circle that fits neatly into the basket of a metal or
bamboo steamer.

method continued overleaf...

HOISIN SAUCE WITH CHINESE DUCK PANCAKES
continued...

On a lightly floured work surface, roll a piece of dough into a 15-cm (6-in) disc. Transfer to the baking paper circle and then rub the top with a little sesame oil – use your fingers not a brush. Repeat with the remaining dough balls, oiling and stacking the discs as you go – the oil will stop them sticking when they're cooked.

Lift the stack and paper into the steamer basket. Steam over a pan of boiling water for 6 minutes. Lift the steamer basket off the pan, invert the pancakes onto a plate and peel off the paper.

When the duck is cooked, pull all the meat and skin away from the bones and shred with two forks. To serve, get everyone to spread a little hoisin sauce onto a pancake and add some duck, cucumber, and springs onions. Roll up and enjoy.

KALE & MACKEREL
★
SWEET POTATO PANCAKES

You'll make more pancakes than you need for this recipe
– but, hey, a pancake glut doesn't constitute a problem.
Enjoy the leftovers topped with fried eggs and hot sauce.
Or simply freeze for another time.

 MAKES 8 x 12-cm
(5-in) pancakes

 TAKES 1½ hours

1 medium sweet potato (about
   350g/12oz)
1 tbsp olive oil
1 small onion, finely chopped
sea salt flakes and freshly ground
   black pepper
1 quantity Buttermilk pancake
   batter (page 18)
1 scant tbsp sriracha sauce
   (½ tsp Tabasco also works well)
3 tbsp vegetable oil
1 tbsp butter
4 handfuls cavolo nero or Swiss
   chard, sliced, tough stalks
   discarded
4 mackerel fillets, skin on
lemon wedges, to serve

Preheat the oven to 220°C/425°F/gas 7. Place the whole sweet potato on a baking sheet and roast for 1 hour, or until very soft. Scoop the flesh into a bowl, mash with a fork, and set aside.

While the sweet potato is roasting, heat the olive oil in a frying pan, add the onion and gently fry with a pinch of salt for 10 minutes, or until soft and golden. Add to the mashed sweet potato when ready; mix well and season to taste with salt and black pepper.

Make the buttermilk pancake batter following the method on page 18 and then stir in the sweet potato mixture and the sriracha.

Heat a non-stick frying pan over a medium heat, add 1 tbsp of the vegetable oil, and swirl to coat. Add a dessertspoonful of the batter to make a thick 10-cm (4-in) pancake – spread out a little with the back of a spoon if necessary. Cook for 1–2 minutes until bubbles start to form on top and the underneath is golden. Flip and fry for

method continued overleaf...

★ ★ ★ ★ ★ ★ ★ ★ ★ ★ ★ ★ ★ ★ ★ ★

KALE & MACKEREL SWEET POTATO PANCAKES
continued...

a further 30 seconds–1 minute. Repeat with the remaining batter, transferring the cooked pancakes to a 150°C/300°F/gas 2 oven as you go to keep warm.

When the pancakes are cooked, melt the butter in a pan over a medium–high heat. Add the cavolo nero, season with salt and black pepper, and cook, shaking the pan, until just wilted. Remove from the heat and cover to keep warm.

Pat dry the mackerel fillets using kitchen paper and season generously with salt and black pepper. Wipe out the pancake pan and set it over a medium–high heat. Add enough of the remaining vegetable oil to lightly coat the base and, when fairly hot, add the mackerel, skin-side down. Fry for about 3 minutes, pressing down with a fish slice, until the skin is crisp and golden. Flip and cook for barely 1 minute more, or until just cooked through.

Place two pancakes on each plate, then top with the wilted kale and a mackerel fillet. Serve with lemon wedges.

CRESPELLE

IN BRODO

Crespelle are thin savoury pancakes that are served in a broth, a bit like pasta, in this classic Italian dish. It makes a soothing and light-but-filling meal.

 SERVES 6 (Makes 12)

 TAKES 40 minutes, plus 30 minutes resting

2 litres (4¼ US pints/8½ cups) good-quality homemade chicken stock
2 eggs, lightly beaten
1 quantity Crêpe batter (page 20, not rested at this point)
50g (1¾oz) grated Pecorino, plus extra to serve
1 heaped tbsp finely chopped parsley
a grating of nutmeg
melted butter or vegetable oil, for brushing

Keep the stock on a low heat while you get on with the crespelle.

Whisk the eggs into the crêpe batter, then stir in half the Pecorino along with the parsley and nutmeg. Leave to stand for 30 minutes.

Heat a non-stick frying pan or crêpe pan over a medium heat and brush with butter or oil. Pour a small ladleful of batter into the pan and quickly swirl to cover the base. Cook for 1–2 minutes, until the edges are dry and the underside golden. Flip and cook for 30 seconds more, then transfer to a plate. Repeat with the remaining batter.

Lay a crespella on a work surface and sprinkle with some of the remaining Pecorino. Tightly roll into a cigar shape and cut in half. Repeat with the remaining crespelle. Place two crespelle into each bowl. Ladle over some of the hot broth, sprinkle with the remaining Pecorino and parsley, and serve immediately.

SPINACH & RICOTTA
★
CRESPOLINI

This comforting Italian dish traditionally contains chicken liver – this version omits the offal with delicious results.

SERVES 4

TAKES 1 hour 30 minutes, plus 30 minutes resting

8 crêpes (made following recipe on page 20)

For the béchamel
750ml (1½ pints/3 cups) whole milk
1 onion, peeled and halved
2 bay leaves
60g (2oz) butter, plus extra for greasing
3 heaped tbsp plain (all-purpose) flour
½ tsp mustard powder (optional)
generous grating nutmeg
1½ tsp sea salt flakes
freshly ground black pepper

For the filling
300g (10oz) trimmed Swiss chard leaves, torn and washed in cold water
300g (10oz) well-drained ricotta
2 small eggs, lightly beaten
60g (10oz) grated Parmesan
grated zest ½ lemon
90g (3oz) grated Gruyère

Preheat the oven to 180°C/350°F/gas 4 and butter a 30x20-cm (12x8-in) baking dish.

To make the béchamel, heat the milk, onion, and bay leaves in a pan until steaming but not boiling. Remove from the heat. Melt the butter in a separate pan, add the flour, and stir for 1 minute over a medium heat until bubbling. Remove from the heat and gradually whisk in the warm milk and discard the onion and bay leaves until everything is amalgamated. Return the pan to a low heat, add the mustard powder (if using), nutmeg, and salt and black pepper. Simmer, stirring constantly, until thickened. Remove from the heat, and add more salt and black pepper if needed. Spread the béchamel in the base of the prepared baking dish.

For the filling, place the chard in a large saucepan set over a medium heat, cover and cook for a few minutes until wilted. Drain well and, when cool enough to handle, squeeze out the excess liquid and finely chop. Place in a bowl along with the ricotta, eggs, half the Parmesan, and the lemon zest. Season generously with salt and black pepper and mix well.

Divide the chard and ricotta mixture equally between the crêpes and roll up into parcels. Arrange on top of the béchamel. Sprinkle over the Gruyère and the remaining Parmesan. Bake for 25 minutes, or until the top is golden. Serve with a crisp green salad.

COCONUT PANCAKES WITH
★
STICKY SALMON

The salmon here is sticky and burnished on the outside, while the flesh is meltingly soft and flavoursome. It goes perfectly with the coconut pancakes and crisp vegetables.

MAKES 4 pancakes

TAKES 50 minutes

For the marinade
2 garlic cloves, crushed
5-cm (2-in) piece fresh ginger,
    peeled and grated
2 tbsp mirin
75ml (2½fl oz/⅓ cup) soy sauce
2 tbsp runny honey
1 tsp vegetable oil
1 tsp toasted sesame oil
squeeze lime juice, plus more
    to serve

4 skinless salmon fillets (about
    500g/1lb 2oz), cut into 3-cm
    (1-in) chunks
1 quantity Coconut crêpe batter
    (page 45)
2 tbsp toasted sesame seeds
2 medium carrots, coarsely grated
    or spiralised
1 medium cucumber, cut into
    ribbons with a peeler
handful micro herbs

Mix all the marinade ingredients together in a small bowl. Place the salmon in a large shallow dish, pour over the marinade, and toss to coat. Set aside while you make the pancakes following the method on page 45. Cover loosely with foil to keep warm and set aside while you cook the salmon.

Preheat the grill to high and line a baking sheet with foil. Arrange the salmon in a single layer on the baking sheet, reserving any leftover marinade. Set the oven rack about 5cm (2in) below the grill – you don't want it too close – and grill the salmon for 4 minutes. Turn the pieces over, brush with the remaining marinade, and cook for a further 3–4 minutes, or until just cooked through.

Distribute the salmon equally between the pancakes, top with the sesame seeds, carrots, cucumber and micro herbs. Fold over and serve immediately, with hot sauce if you like.

PICKLED RADISHES WITH
⭐
CRISPY VIETNAMESE PANCAKES

This famous Vietnamese dish is deliciously addictive: the combination of sweet prawns, crispy pancakes, and tangy pickled radishes is heavenly stuff.

  MAKES 4 pancakes

TAKES 25 minutes

For the pancakes
180g (6oz/heaped 1 cup) rice flour
1 tsp ground turmeric
½ tsp sea salt flakes
3 spring onions (scallions),
   finely sliced
100ml (3½fl oz/scant ½ cup)
   coconut milk
1 tsp sesame oil
vegetable oil, for brushing
about 250ml (9fl oz/1 cup)
   sparkling water (still water
   is fine)
200g (7oz) cooked shelled prawns
120g (4oz) bean sprouts
For the pickle
120g (4oz) radishes, finely sliced
2 tsp caster (superfine) sugar
½ tsp sea salt
2 tbsp white wine vinegar

large handful mint leaves and
   handful crisp lettuce leaves,
   to serve

To make the pancakes, whisk together the flour, turmeric, salt, and spring onions. Stir in the coconut milk and sesame oil, and set aside.

Mix all the pickle ingredients together in a bowl and set aside.

Heat a non-stick frying pan over a high heat and brush generously with the vegetable oil. While the pan is heating – you want it very hot – stir the sparkling water into the batter. Pour a small ladleful of the batter into the pan and swirl to coat the base. Quickly scatter one-quarter of the prawns and bean sprouts over half the pancake. Cook for 2–3 minutes until the bottom is crisp and golden then, using a spatula, fold the pancake over to make a half-moon shape. Cook for another 30 seconds or so.

Serve immediately, with some pickled radishes, mint, and lettuce alongside. Repeat with the remaining batter and ingredients.

SWEET POTATO & RICOTTA
★
GRATINATED CRÊPES

Sweet potato, ricotta and sage are a classic flavour combination. Make the crêpes before you start.

  SERVES 6–8

TAKES 1 hour 30 minutes, plus 30 minutes resting

800g (1¾lb) sweet potatoes, peeled and cut into 2-cm (¾-in) cubes
2 tbsp olive oil
sea salt flakes
freshly ground black pepper
For the filling
60ml (2fl oz/¼ cup) olive oil
2 onions, finely chopped
sea salt flakes
2 garlic cloves, finely chopped
200g (7oz) ricotta
70g (2½oz) grated Parmesan
40g (1¼oz) pine nuts, toasted in a dry frying pan
finely grated zest 1 lemon
good grating nutmeg
3 tbsp double cream
For the sage butter
4 tbsp butter
8 large sage leaves
1 tsp lemon juice

8 crêpes (made following the recipes on page 20)

Preheat the oven to 230°C/450°F/gas 8. Spread the sweet potatoes in a single layer in a baking tray, toss with the oil, and sprinkle with salt and black pepper. Roast for 25–30 minutes, or until tender and brown at the edges; shake the tray now and then to prevent burning.

To make the filling, heat the oil in a frying pan, add the onions and a pinch of salt, and gently fry for 8 minutes, or until very soft but not coloured. Add the garlic and fry for 2 more minutes. Set aside to cool. In a mixing bowl, stir together the ricotta, 20g (¾oz) of the Parmesan, and all the remaining filling ingredients, including the cooled onions. Set aside.

For the sage butter, melt the butter in a pan and let it bubble over a medium heat until it turns golden and smells toasty. Add the sage leaves and lemon juice, and set over a very low heat to keep warm.

Preheat the grill to high. Butter a baking dish 30x20cm (12x8in) or similar.

Distribute the ricotta mixture and sweet potatoes between the crêpes and roll up. Transfer to the baking dish as you go. Brush the tops of the pancakes with some of the sage butter and sprinkle with the remaining Parmesan. Grill for 4–5 minutes (about 10cm/4in below the grill), or until golden. Serve hot, with sage butter spooned over, and sharply dressed leaves alongside.

PIZZA CRÊPES WITH
★
JAMON, MANCHEGO & TOMATO

This pizza-style pancake is a total flavour bomb with a
Spanish vibe: dare you to eat just the one.

 MAKES 4 pizza crêpes

TAKES 40 minutes

vegetable oil, for brushing
1 quantity Crêpe batter (page 20)
  – no need to rest
120g (4oz) Serrano ham or thinly
  sliced jamon
320g (11oz) ripe tomatoes,
  chopped
120g (4oz) Manchego, grated
40g (1¼oz) blanched almonds,
  toasted in a dry frying pan and
  chopped
4 small handfuls basil leaves, torn
4 small handfuls mint leaves, torn
smoked paprika, for sprinkling
extra virgin olive oil, for drizzling

Preheat the grill to high. Heat a non-stick,
ovenproof frying pan over a high heat (one with
a 15-cm/6-in base is perfect) and brush with oil.
When hot, pour 125ml (4fl oz/½ cup) batter into
the pan – this will make a pancake much thicker
than a crêpe – and cook for about 2 minutes, until
just set on top and turning golden underneath.

Pull the pan off the heat and spread one-quarter of
the ham and tomatoes over the top, then scatter
over one-quarter of the cheese. Place under the
grill for 3 minutes, or until the cheese starts to
bubble and turn golden. The pancake might be
slightly puffed and golden in patches, too.

Carefully slide the pancake onto a plate. Scatter
with the almonds and herbs, sprinkle with paprika,
and drizzle with extra virgin olive oil. Serve
immediately and repeat with the remaining batter
and ingredients.

POLISH PANCAKES WITH
★
PAN-FRIED HAKE & AIOLI

This is posh fish and chips: crispy potato pancakes with tender white fish and garlicky lemon mayonnaise. Tuck in.

 SERVES 4

TAKES 30 minutes

For the hake
4 boneless hake fillets, skin on
sea salt flakes
freshly ground black pepper
2 tbsp olive oil

For the aioli
120ml (4fl oz/½ cup) good-
    quality mayonnaise
1 garlic clove, crushed
finely grated zest and juice
    ½ lemon

For the pancakes
500g (1lb 2oz) potatoes
1 small onion, grated
1 egg, lightly beaten
1 tbsp plain (all purpose) flour
sea salt flakes
freshly ground black pepper
small handful parsley, chopped
2 tbsp butter
2 tbsp olive oil

Pat the fish dry with kitchen paper and season generously on both sides with salt and black pepper. Set aside, lightly covered with greaseproof paper.

Combine the aioli ingredients in a small bowl and chill until needed.

For the pancakes, peel and grate the potatoes, putting them in a bowl of iced water as you go. Drain, then squeeze out as much liquid as possible. Place in another bowl, add all the remaining pancake ingredients, except the butter and oil, and mix well. Melt half the butter and half the oil in a frying pan. When foaming, add a large spoonful of the potato mixture to the pan, flattening slightly to make a pancake roughly 8cm (3in) in diameter. Repeat. Fry in batches of 4 for 2–3 minutes on each side over a medium heat, until golden and cooked through. Transfer to a 150°C/300°F/gas 2 oven to keep warm.

To cook the fish, set a frying pan over a medium–high heat, add a splash of oil and wipe it over the base using a wodge of kitchen paper to remove any excess. When the pan is hot, add the fish skin-side down and press the flesh firmly with a fish slice – this helps achieve a lovely crisp skin. Cook for 3–4 minutes, depending on the thickness of the fillet, then flip and cook for 1–2 minutes more.

Serve a fish fillet and two pancakes per person, with the aioli on the side. Serve with steamed green vegetables.

POTATO PANCAKES
★
AVOCADO & PULLED CHICKEN

Pulled pork is a beautiful thing, but can take a gazillion hours to cook. This smoky chicken version is simpler, quicker and (whisper it) almost as good. Boneless chicken thighs are specified for ease, but bone-in works just as well – just remove the bones as you shred.

 SERVES 4 (plus a couple of extra pancakes)

 TAKES 1 hour 45 minutes

2 tbsp olive oil
1 large onion, chopped
sea salt flakes
2 fat garlic cloves, finely chopped
2 tbsp chipotle paste
½ tbsp smoked paprika
½ tbsp cayenne pepper
½ tbsp ground cumin
500g (1lb 2oz) passata
2 tbsp brown sugar
1 tbsp red wine vinegar
6 skinless boneless chicken thighs
1 quantity Potato pancake batter
  (page 28)
2 avocados
soured cream, to serve (optional)

Preheat the oven to 180°C/350°F/gas 4. Heat the oil in an ovenproof pan and fry the onion with a pinch of salt over a medium heat for 5 minutes until softened. Add the garlic and cook for a few minutes more. Stir in the chipotle paste and spices, and fry for 2 minutes. Add the passata, sugar, vinegar, and 150ml (5fl oz/generous ½ cup) cold water and stir well. Gently simmer for 5 minutes. Remove from the heat, add the chicken thighs, poking them under the sauce, and cover. Transfer to the oven and bake for 1 hour, or until the chicken is very tender and almost falling apart.

While the chicken is cooking, fry the potato pancakes following the method on page 28 and keep warm.

When the chicken is ready, lift the pieces out of the sauce onto a chopping board and shred with two forks. Transfer the meat to a bowl and stir in enough of the spicy cooking sauce to coat generously. Taste for seasoning and add more salt if needed.

Just before serving, slice the avocados. To serve, place two pancakes on each plate and top with a generous scoop of the pulled chicken and the avocado slices. Add a dollop of soured cream if you like.

CRÊPE WRAPS WITH
★
SMOKY STEAK & SALSA

Cook the steak on the barbecue if you have the weather
for it. You want the grill searing hot to char the meat.

 SERVES 4–6

TAKES 1 hour 30 minutes,
plus 1 hour marinating

600g (1lb 5oz) hanger (onglet)
  steaks, or similar, 2cm (¾in) thick
For the marinade
juice 2 limes
1 tsp each oregano, cumin, smoked
  paprika, and chilli powder
1 tbsp chipotle paste
1 tsp sea salt flakes
For the salsa
25g (scant 1oz) coriander (cilantro)
  leaves and tender stems, chopped
25g (scant 1oz) parsley leaves and
  tender stems, chopped
2 red chillies, deseeded and finely
  sliced
3 garlic cloves, crushed
2½ tbsp white wine vinegar
½ tsp fish sauce
7 tbsp olive oil
½ tsp sea salt flakes

1 quantity cooked Crêpes (page 20)
garlic-infused olive oil, or plain
  extra virgin olive oil, for brushing
chopped tomatoes, to serve

Cut the steaks across the grain into 8-cm (3-in)
wide strips. Place in a single layer in a shallow bowl.
Whisk together the marinade ingredients, pour
over the steaks, and massage in well. Cover with
clingfilm (plastic wrap) and chill for at least 1 hour.
Return to room temperature before cooking.

Meanwhile, combine the salsa ingredients in a bowl
and set aside.

Lightly brush the crêpes on both sides with the
garlic-infused oil. Heat a chargrill pan until very hot,
and cook the crêpes for about 1 minute on each
side to achieve nice charred stripes.

Wipe the pan and return to the heat. When searing
hot, remove the steaks from the marinade, shaking
off any excess, and cook for 1 minute. Turn the
steaks over and cook for 3 minutes more, turning
the steaks every 30 seconds or so. Set aside,
covered loosely with foil, for 5 minutes.

Finely slice the steaks across the grain. Place a heap
in the centre of each pancake, top with the salsa
and some chopped tomatoes and roll up. Serve
immediately.

TOAD

IN THE HOLE

Use good-quality sausages to make this comforting
dish extra special – spicy Italian ones with a bit
of a chilli kick are fab.

 SERVES 2–4

 TAKES 40 minutes

2 eggs
1 quantity Crêpe batter (page 20)
3 tbsp lard or dripping
8 good-quality sausages

Preheat the oven to 220°C/425°F/gas 7. Whisk the
eggs into the crêpe batter and set aside.

Heat the lard or dripping in a large ovenproof frying
pan – 23cm (9in) diameter is about right – or a
medium baking dish that works on the hob. Add
the sausages and brown them all over.

With the pan or dish still on the heat, pour in the
crêpe batter – be careful, as the fat might spit –
then quickly transfer to the oven.

Bake for about 35 minutes, or until risen and
golden. This is lovely served with onion gravy or
tomato ketchup.

SWEET

★

THINGS

MASCARPONE CREAM

★

BLUEBERRY BLINTZ

A *blintz* generally refers to a crêpe wrapped around a filling. This version is stuffed with a decadent mascarpone cream and topped with berries simmered in just a hint of rosewater. Heavenly.

 MAKES 10 blintz

 TAKES 1 hour, plus 30 minutes resting

1 quantity cooked Crêpes (page 20), loosely covered with foil to keep warm

For the blueberry compote
500g (1lb 2oz) blueberries
100g (3½oz/scant ½ cup) caster (superfine) sugar, or more to taste
2 tbsp lemon juice
1 tsp cornflour (cornstarch)
½ tsp rosewater

For the mascarpone cream
250g (9oz) mascarpone
250ml (9fl oz/1 cup) double cream
1 tbsp icing (confectioner's) sugar
1 tsp vanilla extract

Place all the ingredients for the compote in a pan. Lightly squash the blueberries using a potato masher, then stir over a medium heat until the sugar has dissolved and the berries are starting to release their juices. Gently simmer for 15 minutes or so to make a thick sauce. Remove from the heat and set aside to keep warm.

To make the cream, briefly whisk the mascarpone to loosen. Add the cream, then whisk until light and fluffy. Stir in the icing sugar and vanilla.

To serve, spoon some of the mascarpone cream along the centre of a crêpe and roll up. Spoon over some of the blueberry compote and serve immediately.

CHESTNUT PANCAKES WITH ★ RICOTTA & HONEY

Known as *necci* in Italy, these pancakes are sweet and slightly earthy from the chestnut flour, and make a simple and elegant dessert.

 MAKES 8

 TAKES about 1 hour

For the crêpes
100g (3½oz/¾ cup) chestnut flour
pinch salt
½ tbsp olive oil
melted butter or vegetable oil,
    for brushing
For the filling
400g (14oz) ricotta
1 heaped tbsp dark brown
    soft sugar

runny honey, to serve

To make the crêpes, sift the flour into a mixing bowl and add the salt. Gradually stir in 200ml (7fl oz/generous ¾ cup) cold water and the olive oil to make a smooth batter the consistency of single cream. Set aside.

To make the filling, beat the ricotta and sugar together until well combined and creamy, and chill until needed.

Heat a non-stick frying pan over a medium heat and brush generously with melted butter or oil. Pour 60ml (2fl oz/¼ cup) batter into the pan and quickly swirl to coat. Adjust the heat as needed; these pancakes need to cook slowly or they will burn. When the crêpe begins to look dry on top, after about 4 minutes, loosen the edges using a palette knife and, when golden underneath, flip. Cook for a further couple of minutes. Transfer to a plate covered loosely with foil to keep warm, and cook the remaining batter.

Spread some of the ricotta onto each pancake, roll up and drizzle with honey. Serve immediately.

CHOCOLATE & BERRY-STUFFED
★
PIKELETS

Sneaky. Inside these tender, spongy pancakes is a
hidden trove of melted chocolate and berries. No-one
will ever know.

 MAKES about 4 pikelets

TAKES 30 minutes

vegetable oil, for brushing
1 quantity Pikelet batter (page 26)
handful blueberries
60g (2oz) dark chocolate, ideally
  in 10g (⅓ oz) squares

Heat a non-stick frying pan over a medium heat
and brush with oil. Drop dessertspoonfuls of the
batter into the pan to make 8-cm (3-in) pikelets.
Cook for 30 seconds–1 minute.

Working quickly, drop a few blueberries into the
centre of each pikelet and top with a chocolate
square. Spoon just enough batter on top to cover
the chocolate and blueberries. Cook for a further
1 minute or so until golden underneath – make sure
the heat is not too high or they will burn before
they cook through. Flip and cook for a further
2 minutes.

Delicious served warm while the chocolate is oozy,
but also mighty fine at room temperature.

CHOCOLATE
★
PANCAKE CAKE

OK, so you need to cook an absurd number of pancakes for this cake – but, truly, you get into a comforting rhythm and the results are impressive. And very chocolatey.

Makes 1 cake (Serves 12–16)

TAKES about 2 hours, plus 1 hour resting and cooling

30 cooked crêpes (about 3 quantities Crêpe batter (page 20))
For the chocolate filling
300ml (10fl oz/1¼ cups) double (heavy) cream
300g (10½oz) mix of dark/milk chocolate, chopped
pinch salt
golden syrup, to taste (optional)
For the chocolate glaze
200ml (7fl oz/generous ¾ cup) double (heavy) cream
100g (3½oz) mix of dark/milk chocolate
pinch salt
golden syrup, to taste (optional)

Make the filling by pouring the cream into a pan and heat until almost boiling. Pull the pan off the heat, add the chocolate and salt, and stir until completely combined. Have a taste and add some golden syrup to sweeten (if using). Set aside to cool and thicken.

To assemble the cake, use a palette knife to spread a thin layer of the filling over each pancake, stacking them into a tower on a plate as you go. If you're striving for neatness, stamp out perfect pancake circles using the ring of a 20-cm (8-in) loose-bottom cake tin. Insert the base into the tin, and then stack the chocolate-covered pancakes inside as you go. Transfer to the fridge to chill and set for 30 minutes.

Now, slide the cake onto a wire rack set over a tray or baking sheet (releasing it from the tin if you've used one) – an egg slice is useful to do this. To make the glaze, heat the cream as you did for the filling, add the chocolate and salt, and stir to combine. Add golden syrup to taste (if using). Leave to cool a little – you need the glaze to be thin enough to pour but thick enough to coat the pancakes. Pour the glaze over the pancake stack so that it runs downs and covers the sides. Chill to set.

Serve in modest slices with whipped cream or crème fraîche on the side.

COCONUT PANCAKES

★

PASSION FRUIT CURD

It's gone all tropical here, with mouth-puckering passion fruit and backnotes of coconut. This recipe will make more passion fruit curd than you need, but this a good thing: simply store leftovers in a jar in the fridge for slathering on everything from toast to pavlova.

 MAKES 10 pancakes

 TAKES 45 minutes, plus 30 minutes resting

1 quantity Coconut crêpe batter (page 45)
coconut yoghurt, to serve
For the passion fruit curd
12 passion fruits
150g (5oz) unsalted butter, melted
150g (5oz/¾ cup) caster (superfine) sugar
3 eggs, plus 3 extra yolks, lightly beaten

Make the crêpes following the method on page 45 and cover loosely with foil to keep warm.

For the curd, scoop the passion fruit pulp out of the fruit into a small pan and gently warm through over a medium heat. Pour the pulp into a sieve set over a bowl and push it through with the back of a spoon to separate the seeds. Discard the seeds.

Place the seedless pulp and the remaining curd ingredients in a heatproof bowl set over a pan of gently simmering water, and stir constantly for about 15 minutes until the mixture thickens to a custard consistency. The curd will thicken more as it cools.

Serve the coconut pancakes warm with the curd spooned over, topped with a dollop of coconut yoghurt.

DUTCH PANCAKE WITH
★
RHUBARB & ORANGE CREAM

Simple pancake batter is transformed into a fancy-pants
dessert here, with the tang of blushing rhubarb enhanced
by a cloud of orange-scented cream. It's lovely served
family style – that is, carried ceremoniously to the table
and served straight from the pan.

 SERVES 6

TAKES 1 hour 30 minutes

For the rhubarb
400g (14oz) rhubarb, chopped into
    5-cm (2-in) pieces (very thick
    pieces halved lengthways)
60g (2oz/¼ cup) caster (superfine)
    sugar
2 tbsp orange juice
For the pancake
1 tbsp vegetable oil
100g (3½oz/¾ cup) plain
    (all-purpose) flour
30g (1oz) ground almonds
1 tbsp caster (superfine) sugar
pinch salt
3 eggs, lightly beaten
300ml (10fl oz/1¼ cups) whole
    milk
1 tsp almond extract
1 tsp vanilla extract
1 tbsp butter, melted and cooled

Preheat the oven to 200°C/400°F/gas 6. Place all
the ingredients for the rhubarb in a baking dish
and toss to coat. Roast for 20 minutes, or until the
rhubarb is tender but still holds its shape. Set aside
and increase the oven temperature 220°C/425°F/
gas 7.

To make the pancake, pour the oil into a large
non-stick ovenproof frying pan and place inside the
oven to heat.

In a mixing bowl, whisk together the flour, ground
almonds, sugar, and salt. In a jug, whisk together the
eggs, milk, almond and vanilla extracts and melted
butter. Gradually stir the wet ingredients into the
dry, incorporating the flour as you go to make a
smooth batter: don't overbeat as some small lumps
are fine.

ingredients and method continue overleaf...

★ ★ ★ ★ ★ ★ ★ ★ ★ ★ ★ ★ ★ ★ ★ ★

★ ★

DUTCH PANCAKE WITH RHUBARB & ORANGE CREAM

continued...

1 tbsp icing (confectioner's) sugar,
   for dusting
For the orange cream
300ml (10fl oz/1¼ cups) double
   (heavy) cream
1 tbsp icing (confectioner's) sugar
finely grated zest 1 orange

Working quickly (but carefully!), remove the frying pan from the oven and pour the batter into the hot oil. Return the pan to the oven and bake for 25–30 minutes until puffed, golden, and just cooked through.

While the pancake is cooking, softly whip the cream with the sugar and orange zest.

When cooked, spoon the rhubarb into the centre of the pancake and lightly dust with sifted icing sugar. Serve slices of the pancake from the pan, with spoonfuls of the orange cream on top.

KAISERSCHMARRN WITH
★
TIPSY CHERRIES

This Austrian dessert, made with shredded fluffy pancakes, was named after emperor Franz Joseph I, who apparently couldn't get enough of the stuff. Hats off to him.

 SERVES 4

 TAKES 1 hour, plus
20 minutes soaking

150g (5oz) dried cherries
80ml (2½fl oz/⅓ cup) brandy
   or apple juice
130g (4½oz/1 cup) plain
   (all-purpose) flour
pinch salt
4 eggs, separated
220ml (8fl oz/scant 1 cup)
   whole milk
1 tsp vanilla extract
60g (2oz/¼ cup) caster
   (superfine) sugar
2 tbsp butter, plus extra
   for greasing
1 heaped tbsp demerara sugar,
   for sprinkling
vanilla ice cream, to serve

For the cherry sauce
250g (9oz) fresh cherries
generous squeeze lemon juice
2 tbsp (2oz/⅛ cup) caster
   (superfine) sugar

Preheat the oven to 180°C/350°F/gas 4.

Place the dried cherries in a small bowl, pour over the brandy or apple juice, and set aside to soak for 20 minutes. Drain the soaking liquid in a small pan, and set the cherries aside.

Working over the pan of cherry soaking liquid, remove the stones from the fresh cherries – you'll catch the cherry juice in the pan as you go. Tear the cherries into pieces and drop them into the pan. Add the lemon juice and sugar, and stir. Simmer over a medium heat for 15 minutes, or until reduced and thickened. Set aside.

In a mixing bowl, whisk together the flour and salt, and make a well in the centre. In a jug, whisk together the egg yolks, milk, vanilla, and 3 tablespoons of the caster sugar. Gradually whisk the egg mixture into the dry ingredients, incorporating the flour as you go, to make a smooth batter. Whisk the egg whites to stiff peaks, then whisk in the remaining caster sugar.

method continued overleaf...

★ ★ ★ ★ ★ ★ ★ ★ ★ ★ ★ ★ ★ ★ ★

KAISERSCHMARRN WITH TIPSY CHERRIES
continued...

Gently fold the whites into the batter.

Heat 1 tablespoon of the butter in a frying pan until foaming, then quickly pour in the batter and sprinkle over the soaked, drained dried cherries. Transfer to the oven and bake for 10 minutes, or until golden, puffed, and firm on top – the pancake should only just be cooked through.

Set the grill to high and grease a small baking dish with butter. Using two forks, shred the pancake into pieces and transfer to the baking dish. Dot with the remaining butter and sprinkle with the demerara sugar. Place under the grill for 3–5 minutes, or until the top is crisp and golden.

Serve hot with the cherry compote spooned over and a scoop of vanilla ice cream.

CRÊPES

SUZETTE

Dust off the dessert trolley and ready the cheese and pineapple hedgehogs – we're off to a 1970's dinner party. Jokes aside, this is actually a fantastic dessert, whatever the decade.

SERVES 4–6

TAKES 1 hour 20 minutes, plus 30 minutes resting

1 quantity cooked Crêpes (page 20)

For the sauce
60g (2oz) butter, melted
2 tbsp caster (superfine) sugar
200ml (7fl oz/generous ¾ cup) freshly squeezed orange juice
grated zest 1 orange
3 tbsp Cointreau or Grand Marnier, plus 3 extra tbsp to flambé, if desired

To make the sauce, melt the butter in a large frying pan over a medium–low heat. Whisk together the sugar, orange juice, orange zest, and the 3 tablespoons of alcohol, and pour into the frying pan with the butter. Very gently simmer until the sugar dissolves and the sauce turns slightly syrupy. Slip a crêpe into the sauce, poking it under so it's nicely coated, then fold into a triangle using a spatula. Transfer to a plate, then repeat with the rest of the crêpes. Return the crêpes to the frying pan, again poking them under the sauce, to warm through over a low heat.

To flambé the crêpes, heat the remaining alcohol in a small pan and carefully ignite with a long match – at the table, if you fancy being theatrical. Pour the flaming liquid over the crêpes. When the flames have subsided, serve the crêpes immediately with the sauce spooned over.

PEARS & WALNUTS

★

SALTED CARAMEL CRÊPES

A dessert for those who love salted caramel so much they could drown in it. The pears provide a little fresh contrast to all that buttery caramel, slightly salty goodness.

 SERVES 4 generously

 TAKES 1 hour 10 minutes, plus 30 minutes resting

For the pears
4 pears (about 185g/6½oz) each
1–2 tbsp butter
crème fraîche, to serve

For the caramel
160g (5½oz/¾ cup) light brown soft sugar
1 tbsp golden syrup
120ml (4fl oz/½ cup) double (heavy) cream
1 tsp vanilla extract
2 tbsp butter
½ tsp sea salt flakes, or more to taste
splash rum (optional)

1 quantity cooked Crêpes (p20), kept warm loosely covered under foil
handful toasted walnuts, chopped, and crème fraîche, to serve

Start with the pears. Peel and cut the pears into eighths lengthways and remove the core. Melt 1 tablespoon of the butter in a large frying pan until foaming, then add the pears and reduce the heat to medium–high. Cook for about 6 minutes, turning often, until golden and just tender. Add more butter to the pan if needed. Remove the pan from the heat and set aside.

For the caramel, whisk together the sugar, golden syrup, and 50ml (1¾fl oz/scant ¼ cup) cold water in a pan off the heat. Set the pan over a medium heat and cook, stirring, until the sugar dissolves. Simmer for 3 minutes. Remove the pan from the heat and slowly pour in the cream, stirring constantly, then add the vanilla. Stir in the butter, salt, and rum (if using). Simmer for 5 minutes, stirring, until thickened – the sauce will thicken further as it cools.

Fold the crêpes into quarters and divide between serving plates. Distribute the pears and walnuts on top and drizzle over some of the caramel sauce. Serve with crème fraîche, with extra sauce on the table for those who want more.

DOUBLE CHOCOLATE
★
RYE PANCAKES

Rye flour for depth of flavour plus chocolate bits for decadent gooeyness equals obscenely good pancakes. Drizzle over chocolate glaze (from the chocolate pancake cake recipe on page 148) if your chocolate itch really needs scratching, otherwise a cooling, tart splodge of crème fraîche works beautifully.

MAKES 8 pancakes

TAKES 35 minutes

150g (5oz/1¼ cups) rye flour
3 tbsp cocoa powder
1½ tsp baking powder
3 tbsp dark brown soft sugar
pinch salt
1 egg, lightly beaten
270ml (9½fl oz/generous 1 cup) whole milk
1 tbsp melted butter
80g (3oz) good-quality dark chocolate in your flavour of choice (orange and almond, butterscotch, chilli or hazelnut work well), chopped, plus extra grated chocolate to serve
melted butter or vegetable oil, for brushing
crème fraîche, to serve

Whisk together the flour, cocoa powder, baking powder, sugar, and salt in a mixing bowl. Break up any lumps of sugar with the back of a spoon. Make a well in the centre. In a jug, whisk together the egg, milk, and melted butter. Gradually stir the wet ingredients into the dry, incorporating the flour as you go, to make a thick, smooth batter. Fold in the chopped chocolate.

Heat a non-stick frying pan over a medium heat and brush with butter or oil. Pour 60ml (2fl oz/ ¼ cup) batter into the pan and cook for 1–2 minutes, or until bubbles appear on top. Make sure the pan is not too hot or the chocolate will burn before the pancakes are cooked through. Flip and cook for a further minute or so. Transfer to a plate and cover loosely with foil to keep warm while you repeat with the rest of the batter.

Serve warm with a spoonful of crème fraîche and some grated chocolate sprinkled over.

GINGERBREAD

★

PANCAKES

The spices and treacle make these taste a bit like
Christmas, but they make a perfect afternoon tea treat
anytime of year, especially spread with a slick of butter
and/or a puddle of golden syrup.

 MAKES 10 pancakes

TAKES 30 minutes

150g (5oz/1¼ cups) plain
　(all-purpose) flour
1 tsp baking powder
½ tsp bicarbonate of soda
2 tbsp dark brown soft sugar
pinch salt
1 tsp ground ginger
2 tsp ground cinnamon
a pinch ground cloves
1 egg, lightly beaten
250ml (9fl oz/1 cup) buttermilk
1 tbsp treacle
1 tbsp butter, melted and cooled
　slightly
melted butter or vegetable oil,
　for frying

Whisk together the flour, baking powder,
bicarbonate of soda, sugar, salt, and spices in mixing
bowl. In a separate bowl, whisk together the egg,
buttermilk, treacle, and melted butter. Make a well
in the centre of the dry ingredients and gradually
pour in the egg mixture, whisking as you go to
incorporate the flour to make a thick batter. Don't
over mix.

Heat a non-stick frying pan over a medium heat
and brush with butter or oil. Pour 60ml (2fl oz/¼
cup) batter into the pan and cook for 1–2 minutes,
or until starting to bubble on top. Flip and cook
for a further 30 seconds–1 minute until golden
underneath. Repeat with rest of batter. Best
served warm.

MAPLE APPLE
★
OVEN PANCAKE

Decadent and moreish, this heavenly dessert is a bit like a tarte Tatin, but simpler to make, as the pancake batter is far less of a headache than pastry. The apples and maple syrup combo is an absolute winner.

  SERVES 6

TAKES 50 minutes

2 tbsp caster (superfine) sugar
1 tsp vanilla extract
1 quantity Buttermilk pancake batter (page 18)
5 medium eating apples
60g (2oz) butter
90ml (3fl oz/⅓ cup) maple syrup
squeeze lemon juice
250ml (9fl oz/1 cup) double (heavy) cream
1 tsp ground cinnamon

Preheat the oven to 220°C/425°F/gas 7. Stir the sugar and vanilla into the pancake batter and set aside.

Peel, core, and quarter the apples, then cut each quarter in half (or quarters if large). Melt the butter until foaming in an ovenproof frying pan, with a 15-cm (6-in) diameter base, add the apples, maple syrup, and lemon juice, and stir to combine. Simmer over a medium heat for about 10 minutes until the apples have softened and the liquid has reduced to a syrup: there should be plenty of syrup in the pan by end of cooking.

Pull the pan off the heat, spread the pancake batter over the top with a spatula, making sure it completely covers the apples. Bake in the preheated oven for about 15 minutes, until golden and cooked through. Meanwhile, whip with the cream and cinnamon together in a small bowl.

When the pancake is cooked, carefully invert it onto a plate. Cut into slices and serve warm with a generous spoonful of the cinnamon cream.

PUFFED PANCAKE WITH
★
APRICOTS & ALMONDS

Pretty as a picture, the pale-orange apricot pieces peep
through the top of this giant pancake most beguilingly.

 SERVES 6

 TAKES 1 hour

2 eggs
½ tsp almond extract
2 tbsp caster (superfine) sugar
1 quantity Crêpe batter (p20)
For the apricots
350g (12½oz) apricots, stoned
   and halved
2 tbsp caster (superfine) sugar
30g (1oz) butter
1 tbsp toasted flaked almonds,
   to serve
sifted icing (confectioner's) sugar,
   for dusting

Preheat the oven to 220°C/425°F/gas 7. Whisk the
eggs, almond extract, and sugar into the crêpe
batter and set side.

Meanwhile, prepare the apricots. In a mixing bowl,
toss the apricots with the sugar. Heat the butter
in a large ovenproof frying pan until foaming, then
add the apricots. Cook over a medium–high heat
for about 8 minutes, shaking the pan frequently,
until almost tender. Increase the heat to high for
1 minute or so, then pour in the pancake batter.
Transfer to the oven and bake for 25–30 minutes,
or until puffed, golden, and cooked through. To
serve, sprinkle with the almonds and lightly dust
with sifted icing sugar.

INDEX

THANK YOU

Thanks to everyone at Quadrille for
making this beautiful book happen,
especially Sarah: opportunities to cook
and eat pancakes 24/7 don't come
along every day! Thanks also to my
home squad, Adam, Ruby and Ben, for
all your feedback and last-minutes
dashes to the shops.